REPORT CARD
ON BASAL READERS

Authors and Researchers:

Kenneth S. Goodman, University of Arizona
Patrick Shannon, York University
Yvonne Freeman, Fresno Pacific College
Sharon Murphy, Newfoundland
   Department of Education

RICHARD C. OWEN PUBLISHERS, INC.,   Katonah, New York

This is a report prepared by the Reading Commission (Dorothy Watson, Director) of the National Council of Teachers of English. It was originally presented for response and review at the Invitational Conference on the Basal Reader, Los Angeles, November 23 and 24, 1987. Research for this report was supported under a grant from the NCTE Research Foundation. Publication of this report does not constitute an endorsement of the findings or recommendations by NCTE or the NCTE Research Foundation.

RICHARD C. OWEN PUBLISHERS, INC.
135 Katonah Avenue
Katonah, New York 10536

PRINTED IN THE UNITED STATES OF AMERICA

Book design by Ken Venezio

Preface

The American people, more than any other people in the world, have a deeply ingrained belief that technology, in and of itself, can solve human problems. In education this technology is not yet machine-based. It is a technology of texts and tests. Both the public and the educational profession have come to accept tests and textbooks as an infallible technology, the product of the best that science has to offer. In no other aspect of education does this total trust in technology reach the level that it does in reading instruction. And this is no accident, since the technology of reading lessons is embodied in a huge brightly illustrated package, the basal reader, which makes an attractive promise to all concerned with reading instruction in America. Basal publishers have convinced most reading experts and many school officials that basal programs are sequential all-inclusive sets of instructional materials which can teach all children to read, *if* teachers will follow the di-

rections in the basal teachers' manual. The promise is
that, when used faithfully, the basal technology will
solve the problem of developing universal literacy for
all Americans. Few have been able to resist the promise
and the sparkling packaging of basal readers.

Basals are now so dominant that they have become
the reading curriculum in nearly all schools. So strong
is the trust in the basal technology that both teachers'
and students' performance are judged by the basal
manuals and their objective referenced tests. When
children fail to learn to read easily and well through
basal instruction the blame goes either to the teacher
for not following the basal carefully or to the children
as disabled learners. Teachers who have carefully followed the detailed manuals of the basals are told that
the fault if learners fail is in the learners. Another technology, the technology of reading disability, is then
evoked to remediate these defective learners. In many
American schools promotion from one grade to another is largely based on success or failure in the basals.
Rarely are lesson content and instructions examined for
their possible contribution to the students' problems.
Both teachers and pupils become dependent on the
basal materials during reading lessons (*see* Shannon,
1988 for an extended discussion).

It is the absolute dominance of basal readers that led
the Commission on Reading of the National Council of
Teachers of English to initiate this study into basal
reading programs. This is a report to the profession
and the general public. The concern of the Commission
is with the promotion of literacy in the United States.
Toward that end *Report Card on Basal Readers* takes an
advocate's position in favor of students and teachers as
we seek to answer many questions: Why do teachers
and students find themselves in a position of power-
lessness during reading instruction? Who benefits and

who suffers from the present reading programs? What are the consequences of perpetuating the status quo? How possible is change toward greater freedom for teachers in control of their teaching and for students in control of their learning and literacy.

This report examines the nature of the modern basal, its economics and use. First, a history is provided showing how the confluence of business principles, positivistic science and behavioral psychology led to the transformation of reading textbooks into basal readers. Next, the report examines objective and subjective factors which maintain the dominance in American reading instruction of a small number of very large publishers through their basal readers. The economics and ethics of marketing basals are also examined. Then, the process of producing basals is described, drawing on investigative reporting. That leads to a thorough examination of contemporary basals using a descriptive instrument. Finally, we offer our recommendations for progress in reading instruction within and without the basals. While we have tried to be fair in this report we have not tried to be neutral. We are concerned for what is good or bad for learners and the teachers trying to help them become literate. For too long, professional criticism of basal readers has been muted and restrained. In this *Report Card* we have opened them up for all to see.

January, 1988   Kenneth S. Goodman
                                   Patrick Shannon
                                   Yvonne Freeman
                                   Sharon Murphy

Acknowledgments

Pamela Babcock coordinated the work for this report over much of its history. Other important contributions were made by Carol Gile, Carol Christine, Jane Flurky, Nancy Fries, Yetta Goodman, Shiela Nicholas, Danjuma Salawa, and Kathleen Shannon.

The writers are grateful for the support of the members of the NCTE Commission on Reading (1986-7) who read, critiqued, and approved the original draft. These were Dorothy Watson, Director, University of Missouri; David Bloome, University of Massachusetts; Marilyn Boutwell, Teachers College, Columbia University; Robert F. Carey, Rhode Island College; Paul Crowley, Columbia Missouri Schools; Barbara M. Flores, California State University, San Bernardino; Peter H. Fries, Central Michigan University; Kenneth S. Goodman, University of Arizona; Karla F.C. Holloway, North Carolina State University; Angela Jagger, New York University; Vera E. Milz, Bloomfield Hills Schools; Karl Koenke, NCTE Liaison.

We are also grateful to the almost 200 people who attended the invitational conference on the basal reader held in November 1987 in connection with the NCTE convention in Los Angeles. Their discussion, and the written comments several later offered, were extremely useful in the revision of the draft report. We greatly appreciate those who served on panels at the conference: Publishers and Editors James Squire, John McInnis, and Philip LaLeike; Teachers Debra Goodman, Vera Milz, Karen Smith; Administrators Margaret Stevenson, Carol Kuykendahl, Francie Alexander; Researchers Rand Spiro, Judith Greene, and Yetta Goodman; Literature and Language Theorists Rudine Sims and Jerome Harste; Authors Jean Greenlaw, Rosalinda Barrera, and Margaret Early. P. David Pearson, David Bloome, and Rosemary Hiller spoke at an open meeting of the conference. Constance Weaver provided the closing remarks at the conference. As current director of the Commission on Reading, she has been a great support in the revision and publication of this report. Carol Gile, Kathy O'Brien, Christine Moore, Pamela Babcock, Mary Bixby, and Wendy Kasten recorded and summarized the discussion for our use in revision.

—K.S.G.
P.S.
Y.F
S.M.

Contents

1

THE CENTRAL PREMISE OF THE BASAL READER

The central premise of the basal reader is that a sequential, all-inclusive set of instructional materials can teach all children to read *regardless of teacher competence* and *regardless of learner differences*. It is all-inclusive in the sense that basals claim to include *everything* that any learner needs to learn to read (the *scope* of the basal). It presents this all inclusive program organized around a hierarchy of skills and a tightly controlled vocabulary (the *sequence* of the basal). A promise is made to administrators that the basal eliminates teacher competence as a factor in successful reading development, provided that teachers follow the manual exactly.

Implicit in this premise is that the basal is indispensable to reading instruction, that without it children would either not learn to read at all or would be severely handicapped. More explicit is the claim that everything that is in the program is there, in the specific place in the sequence it is found, for scientific reasons. Many teachers and administrators have come to believe that skipping a single page or exercise could harm pupils in some potentially permanent way.

2

PUTTING THE BASAL IN HISTORICAL CONTEXT

Three generations have read from basals while attending school.

Walk into any elementary classroom and there is a 90 percent chance that you will see students and teachers working with basal readers, workbooks, or teachers' manuals. Although not everyone supports this practice, it has been a fact of American education, and three generations have read from basals while attending school. It may be understandable then that these materials are generally seen today as a necessary part of reading instruction. Few teachers, administrators, or parents have experienced reading instruction without them. How basal materials were developed, rose to their present place of prominence, and what this means for teachers are the main questions addressed in this chapter.

Readering Instruction Before Basal Reading Materials

It's not an easy job to describe reading instruction before the advent of the basal readers in the 1920s because most analyses of reading instruction of that period consider only materials (*e.g.*, Smith, 1965), expert opinion (*e.g.*, Mathews, 1966) or policy (*e.g.*, Cubberly, 1934). As we have recently learned, activity and change at these levels do not always translate into change in the day-to-day interactions among teachers and students—or masters and scholars as they were often called then (Cuban, 1984). Although we run the risk of misrepresenting the actual activities of reading instruction, we only have descriptions of materials and policy for the very early period of American reading instruction.

As early as 1647 the Massachusetts Colony passed a bill ("the Old Deluder, Satan Law") which required townships of over fifty households to appoint a teacher of reading and writing so that children might learn to resist temptation by reading *Bible* verses. Prior to that time, and in other colonies, reading instruction was largely a private, religious matter, and many Americans did not become literate. For example, illiteracy rates in New England in the seventeenth century ranged from 20 to 60 percent according to census data (Soltow & Stevens, 1981). Until the middle of the eighteenth century there were few books for children (Huck, 1976), and the instructional materials for reading of the time included hornbooks (paddles which contained the alphabet [in two scripts], a syllabarium, and the Lord's Prayer all on a 3" x 5" inch surface), psalters (books of spelling lessons, lists of syllables and words, and Bible verses) and textbooks such as *The New England Primer* which began "A—In Adam's fall we sinned all." As best can be determined, memorization of Bible verses was the ultimate goal for most students and teaching methods followed two forms: student's independent practice of lessons following recitation before an overseeing master or the master leading students in choral drills of the lessons.

With John Newbery's *A Little Pretty Pocketbook* in 1744, the publishing of children's books began in earnest. Some of these books were published in North

America during the Revolutionary War. Their contents demonstrated a change in child rearing philosophies from instilling a fear of God to developing a positive moral character within children. Although there is little evidence that this literature was used widely in schools, the instructional materials of the times reflected a similar change in tone. The lessons in Noah Webster's *Blue Backed Speller* were patriotic and morally didactic, and the 1800 edition of *The New England Primer* began "A was an angler who fished with a hook." The goals for education were also modified as suggested in Thomas Jefferson's words: "If a nation expects to be ignorant and free, in a state of civilization, it expects what never was and will never be" (Jefferson, 1893, p. 221). Jefferson proposed universal schooling for all citizens in literacy, arithmetic, and history "at common expense to all" as the primary protection against tyranny.

Jefferson proposed universal schooling for all citizens in literacy, arithmetic, and history...

Perhaps the best source of information of teacher and student interactions in the nineteenth century is Barbara Finkelstein's (1970) *Governing the Young: Teacher's Behavior in American Primary Schools, 1820-1880*, in which she synthesizes almost 1,000 first-hand accounts of teaching practices from students, teachers, and observers. During this period reading instruction emphasized word identification over meaning; required oral reading rather than discussion; and was largely directed by the available textbooks, most of which were developed more according to their author's whim than according to pedagogical principles. Finkelstein concludes:"the descriptive literature suggests that most teachers of reading confined their activities to those of the overseer and drillmaster" (p. 26).

The spelling method predominated in reading instruction; students learned the names of letters (lower case, capital, and italic), spelled them, pronounced lists of two- and three-letter nonsense syllables, and then spelled and pronounced lists of words of various lengths before they began to read sentences orally. In

Webster's American Spelling Book, the most popular textbook of its time, reading of sentences did not begin
until page 101. In schools with students of various
ages, teachers grouped students into classes according
to their ability to spell these lists. The following state-
ments provide a first hand glimpse of first the overseer
technique, which put the burden of learning to read on
the individual students, and of the drillmaster in a so-
called "loud school."

> The class, composed of eight or ten scholars, takes its
> place each one toeing the mark on the floor. The master
> commands "attention," then "obedience." The boys
> bow their heads and the girls curtsey. One end is called
> the head, the other the foot of the class. The teacher
> opens the book, which is of course *Webster's Elementary,*
> and, turning to the lesson, pronounces the words, be-
> ginning at the head. The scholar spells the word, but if
> he or she misspells the word it is given to the next
> one...(J.S. Minard, *Recollections of the Log School House
> Period, 1905).*

> The teacher had an odd contrivance nailed to a post
> set up in the middle of the room. It was known as a
> "spelling board." When he pulled the string to which
> the board was fastened the students gave attention. If
> he let the board halfway down the scholars could spell
> out words in moderate tones. If he pulled the board up
> tight, everybody "spelled to themselves." When he
> gave the cord a pull until the plank dropped down, the
> hubbub began. Everything went with a roar. Just as
> loud as you pleased, you could spell anything. People
> along the road were happy to know the children were
> having their lessons. (R.L. Felton, *County Life in Georgia
> in the Days of My Youth,* 1919).

By the 1860s most urban schools had shifted from an
emphasis on spelling to one of pronunciation, from letter names to their sounds—(however, most rural
schools retained spelling methods (Mathews, 1966).
Lead by McGuffey's *Eclectic First Reader for Young Children* (1836), reading instruction directed children from
letters and their pronunciation to words and then to
simple sentences. To assist in this early phonics instruc-

tion a *McGuffey's Reader* with a modified alphabet was published to overcome the lack of correspondence between symbol and sound in English (*Leigh's McGuffey's New Eclectic Primer in Pronouncing Orthography*, 1868). According to the descriptions in Finkelstein (1970), this phonics method lent itself as easily to a similar practice of oral drill and individual learning as had been experienced with the spelling method.

Despite Horace Mann's advocacy in the 1840s and 1850s, the word method made little headway as a teaching method until the 1870s and 1880s. Finkelstein argues that the method failed to attract teachers' enthusiasm because it required teachers to become "interpreters of culture" rather than overseers or drillmasters. That is, the word method in its pure form eliminated the alphabet, syllabarium, and spelling exercises from textbooks, beginning instead with familiar words complete with discussion of their meaning. Acceptance of the word method, then, required teachers to redefine the goals of education, from the reproduction of the facts within textbooks to the interpretation of those facts (Rice, 1893). However, most teachers who used the word method combined it with a phonics method—pronouncing the word, requiring students to repeat it in unison, breaking it immediately into its phonic elements, blending those sounds to its original pronunciation, and finally discussing its meaning. Finkelstein summarizes reading instruction prior to 1880 by stating:

> The evidence suggests that whether (teachers) taught in urban or rural schools in the North, South, East, or West; whether they instructed students according to the literal, syllabic, or word system, they typically defined reading as reading aloud—an activity which required the teacher to do little more than assign selections to be read, and, if he chose, to correct the pronunciation of his students (p. 49).

Indeed, Joseph Mayer Rice came to this same conclusion during his observation of elementary schools in thirty-six cities in 1892 as the prelude to a series of arti-

Reading instruction in nearly 90 percent of the schools in these cities was out- dated, mechanical, and totally ineffective.

cles for *Forum Magazine*. In the best muckraking tradi- tion Rice reported that reading instruction in nearly 90 percent of the schools in these cities was outdated, me- chanical, and totally ineffective.

> "I found the results in reading and in writing lan- guage almost universally poor in schools where read- ing matter, at least during the first two years, consisted of nothing but empty words, silly sentences, and baby- trash, and where the time spent in writing was devoted to copying such words and sentences from the black- board or the reading book" (p. 26, 1893).

As an example of mechanical instruction, Rice of- fered this observation from a Chicago primary school:

> After entering the room containing the youngest pupils, the principal said to the teacher, "Begin with the mouth movements and go right straight through"...About fifty pupils now began in concert to give utterance to the sounds of a, e, and oo varying their order, thus: a, e, oo, a, e, oo; e, a, oo, etc....When some time had been spent in thus maneuvering the jaw, the teacher remarked, "Your tongues are not loose." Fifty pupils now put out their tongues and wagged them in all directions. The principal compli- mented the children highly on their wagging (p. 176- 77).

Although Rice drew the same general conclusion about reading instruction as Finkelstein had, Rice did not blame teachers alone for the problems as Finkel- stein clearly implied. Rather, Rice spread the blame among unconcerned parents, meddling politicians, uninformed and overworked school superintendents, and poorly educated teachers. While he cajoled parents to take an active part in their children's education, he offered three "laws" that had to be obeyed if schools were to improve:

1. the school system must be absolutely divorced from politics in every sense of the word,
2. the supervision of the schools must be properly directed and thorough....the principal aim of which is to increase the professional strength of the teachers, and

3. the teachers must constantly endeavor to grow both in professional and in general intellectual strength" (p. 17-18).

In contrast to the mechanical schools Rice considered the schools in four cities to be "scientific" and progressive" in their approaches to reading and education in general (the New Education). These schools attempted to implement principles of the "science of education," developed from the study of European philosophers of education (*e.g.*, Rousseau, Pestalozzi, Froebel, and Herbart). This science focused on the study of children's needs and a unification of subjects within a curriculum. Rice argued that in these schools "it is no longer the textbook or the arbitrary will of the superintendent, but the laws of psychology, that now become the ruling spirit of the school" (p. 21).

Concerning the position of reading instruction, Rice stated:

> In schools conducted upon the principles of unification, language is regarded simply as a means of expression and not as a thing apart from ideas. Instruction in almost every branch now partakes of the nature of a language-lesson. The child being led to learn the various phases of language in large part incidentally while acquiring and expressing ideas. . . . strange as it may seem, it is nevertheless true that the results in reading and expression of ideas in writing are, at least in the primary grades, by far the best in those schools where language, in all its phases, is taught incidentally...(p. 223-24).

One of the schools Rice singled out for praise was Cook County Normal, which had been under the direction of Francis Parker for ten years prior to Rice's visit. Already famous for the innovative Quincy System, Parker and his teachers took the word method to its logical conclusion by de-emphasizing the use of textbooks and by emphasizing the utility of literacy in students' lives. Only after the reading habit was well-established were letter sounds introduced, primarily through the slow pronunciation of simple

"It is no longer the textbook or the arbitrary will of the superintendent, but the laws of psychology, that now become the ruling spirit of the school". (Rice)

known words (Mathews, 1966). This shift away from sound and the emphasis on utility also sparked interest in silent reading since it more closely approximated adult reading behaviors (Hyatt, 1943). Of prime importance in Parker's school was the teachers' ability to arouse children's interest sufficiently in a topic that they would willingly learn to read in order to study the topic thoroughly. For Rice, "Of all the schools that I have seen, I know of none that shows so clearly what is implied by an educational ideal as the Cook County Normal School" (p. 209-210).

Combining moral indignation against partisan politics, the public's fascination with science, and optimism about the future, Rice's articles in the *Forum* were generally accepted as fact (Cremin, 1961). Despite educators' protests to the contrary, it was clear to most citizens that schools were unprepared and unable to help Americans adapt to the changes caused by rapid industrialization, urbanization, and immigration. Although there was general agreement concerning the need for change and science as the best tool for that change, there was little agreement concerning solutions. Businessmen sought vocational education and efficiency (Katznelson & Weir, 1985); settlement workers recommended instruction in hygiene and child care (Lagemann, 1985), and "patriots" demanded a curriculum based on American values (Greer, 1972). For the superintendents of schools whose jobs depended on public support, the problem was one of degree —should schools be completely overhauled, abandoning the traditional emphases on teachers and textbooks in order to adopt the New Education's emphases on the child and unified curriculum or should the traditional emphases be technically fine-tuned.

REASONS FOR DEVELOPING BASAL READING MATERIALS

In order to understand why the technical fine-tuning

of traditional reading instruction won out over the unified curriculum of the New Education, it is necessary to digress for a consideration of the spirit of the times in which this crisis in school literacy took place.

During the latter part of the nineteenth century and the early decades of the twentieth, many Americans enjoyed the prosperity brought about by the industrialization of productive means. As a result, they became enamored with businessmen, values, and practices that they believed were responsible for this progress. To be sure, the values of hard work and honesty were inscribed in the instructional materials of the 1800s, but the overwhelming productive change and the fortunes amassed by Carnegie, Rockefeller, Morgan, and the like directed the public's attention to how these principles had been applied successfully in industry and private life. Hierarchical management, efficiency, and the profit motive became the organizational strops used to hone the public institutions of the times.

Hierarchical management, efficiency, and the profit motive became the organizational strops used to hone the public institutions of the times.

In several ways science was also influential in the development of America's institutions. First, it provided a rational explanation for the apparent problems of industrialization. That is, science "dis-enchanted" things of nature by relying on physical rather than metaphysical explanations. Since things were made up of atoms—not spirits—there was little reason to worry about the soul in the environment. And when Darwinism was applied to consideration of inequality in standards of living it explained emotionlessly that this was due to the survival of the fittest. Second, science (understood as technology) seemed to be the driving force of material progress. If science was good for business, the logic went, it must be good for social life also. Third, science promised a rational explanation of any thing or phenomenon through the discovery of its compliance with the laws of nature. These laws in turn were developed by dividing nature into discrete causal variables to be measured quantitatively and thus understood.

The search for a science of education was directed

From the results of his experiments Thorndyke fashioned laws of learning.

primarily by the emergence of the new academic discipline of psychology. Although initial efforts to study the development of mind were informed by the Darwinian notion that ontogeny recapitulates phylogeny, American educational psychology found its most influential and proactive voice in Edward L. Thorndyke. Through his experiments on animals, Thorndyke concluded that learning could be studied by the examination of behavior, because it appeared as the organisms' total response to its environment. As a total response learning could be observed, and the degree of learning measured as an indication of its nature.

Thorndyke's conclusions were more than just a demonstration that psychology could be scientific. With his connection of mind and body through reactive behavior, he simultaneously rejected original sin from the Bible and Rousseau's natural state of grace explanations of human nature, replacing them with the notion that people could learn to be bad or good depending on their environment. Thus Thorndyke challenged the contemporary views of teaching as a battle against the evil within children (traditional emphasis) and as an impediment to children's natural development (New Education emphasis).

From the results of his experiments Thorndyke fashioned laws of learning in which he attempted to describe how knowledge was composed from discrete stimulus and response connections and how teachers could best manage their students' learning environments:

1. From associationist psychologists, he took the notion that learning is ordered, that efficient learning follows one best sequence *(The Law of Readiness)*.
2. From James Watson, Thorndyke accepted the idea that practice strengthens the bond between a stimulus and a response *(The Law of Exercise)*.
3. From his own experiments, he concluded that rewards influenced the stimulus-response connection *(The Law of Effect)*.

4. And from later work, Thorndyke developed the idea that the learning of a particular stimulus-response connection should be tested separately and under the same conditions in which it was learned *(The Law of Identical Elements)*. Indeed, Thorndyke and others developed tests to measure students' progress in the language arts and most other facets of elementary education.

In this ethos of business, science, and psychology the radical changes required to implement the New Education seemed inefficient, sentimental, and overly optimistic concerning human learning. Francis Parker, whom Rice had celebrated at the end of his articles in 1893, was forced to resign from Cook County Normal School in 1899 amid rising public criticism of his pedagogy. Certainly the New Education, as championed by John Dewey and William Kilpatrick generally and by Laura Zirbes in reading, flourished in some school districts; but its major effect came from the ability of some traditionalists to accommodate some of its elements into their methods without threatening traditional educational goals. This ability to incorporate elements of child-centered and textbook-centered instruction is how elementary education has appeared to change over time while essentially remaining the same (Cuban, 1984).

SCIENTIFIC MANAGEMENT

Perhaps the best example of how the spirit of business, science, and psychology came to influence education is found in the development and implementation of scientific management. Born at the turn of the century as a method to increase workers' productivity, and therefore industrialists' profits, scientific management required the analysis of the labor activities of the most able worker so that this model might become standard practice for all workers. To begin, the able worker's procedure was analyzed for its discrete parts; then each part was timed in order to eliminate nonessential movements, and finally these streamlined parts were reassembled into a series of activities performed by groups of workers. These new procedures were learned in a step-by-step fashion, each worker practicing his part while being timed, while financial incentives were offered to those employees who performed their tasks according to these administrative plans. By 1910 scientific management was front page news; in 1911 the National Educational Association's Department of Superintendents (later to become the American Association of School Administrators) appointed the Committee on the Economy of Time in Education; and in 1914 Joseph Mayer Rice published his second book, *Scientific Management in Education.*

The Committee on the Economy of Time was charged with the responsibility of making recommendations to eliminate nonessentials from the elementary curriculum, to improve teaching methods, and to set minimum standards for each subject. Among the Committee members were Frank Spaulding, then Superintendent of Minneapolis Schools, and J.F. Bobbitt, an Assistant Professor of Education at the University of Chicago, both of whom were closely associated with the translation of scientific management to schooling practices (Callahan, 1962). Spaulding and Bobbitt argued for a three-step procedure in order to design instruction scientifically:

1. Analyze the learning environment during instruction to identify instructional methods.
2. Measure the effects of various methods with specifically designed tests.
3. Adopt the methods that yield the highest test results.

This is precisely the approach that the Committee used in their four reports published between 1915 and 1919 as yearbooks for the National Society for the Study of Education (NSSE).

Although William S. Gray became principal spokesman for the Committee concerning reading instruction and research, the survey of contemporary practices in elementary classrooms (the first report) included Robinson Jones' essay on the standardization of vocabulary in textbooks according to its frequency in print, S.A. Courtis' report on minimum standards for reading rates for intermediate grade students, Gray's selected bibliography of reading tests, and James Fleming Hosic's essay on standards for the content in elementary school literature programs (Bagley, 1915). The second report from the Committee included Gray's explanation of the relationship between instructional emphasis on silent reading and economy in education, and O.F. Mesnon's and J.H. Hoshinson's survey of recommended library books and textbooks organized according to grade level (Wilson, 1917). In the third report, E.T. Housh reported on the standard vocabularies in second grade readers (Wilson, 1918); and in the final report (Seashore, 1919), Gray published the "Principles of Method in Teaching Reading, as Derived from Scientific Investigation." In this he enunciated the key criteria on which basals have been constructed ever since. By far, this fourth report was the most widely circulated (Cremin, 1961).

Gray's "Principles" consisted of forty-eight maxims developed from his summary of thirty-five scientific investigations of reading, which covered norms for students' progress across grade levels, suggestions in oral and silent reading instruction, even specifications for the printing of books to maximize economy in reading—all in twenty-six pages. As in the second report, Gray stressed the efficiency, utility, and overall superiority of silent reading in developing students' reading rates and comprehension. Although he acknowledged that oral reading was appropriate for early lessons, Gray adopted a moral tone concerning how it ought to be used: "Oral reading exercises should emphasize the content of what is read" (p. 31); "Two different types of oral reading exercises should be provided for second and third grades" (p. 37); and "The oral reading which

Gray published the "Principles of Method in Teaching Reading, as Derived from Scientific Investigation." In this he enunciated the key criteria on which basals have been constructed ever since.

is required in the fourth, fifth, and sixth grades should be conducted under the stimulus of a real motive" (p. 37). However, Gray returned to scientific authority when he later addressed rate and comprehension: "Much reading of simple interesting materials is effective in increasing rate of reading" (p. 41); and "Knowledge, while reading, that the material is to be reproduced improves the quality of the reading" (p. 41).

Clearly, Gray's essay demonstrates the Committee's intent to change typical reading instruction in public schools, yet a close analysis of Gray's words suggests that the fundamental conditions of traditional reading instruction were to remain the same. Influences of the New Education are present in Gray's rhetoric: "emphasize the content of what is read," "a real motive," etc. However, instruction was to remain teacher-centered; there is virtually no mention of a unified curriculum or even unification of the language arts (writing, handwriting, spelling, and grammar were treated as separate subjects) to further children's interests; and the recitation of passage content was to continue as the goal of reading instruction—"material is to be reproduced." The fine-tuning of these traditions would come when test scores, and not superintendents or teachers, would decide how to teach reading. Surprisingly, the Committee was silent concerning how these modest but numerous changes were to penetrate the classroom door and alter the day-to-day interactions between teachers and students.

Since many elementary schoolteachers were poorly educated, knowledgeable superintendents were in short supply, and teachers already relied heavily on textbooks, changes were suggested through a teachers' manual which was to direct teachers' use of instructional materials. Although some previous textbooks had included brief directions for teachers in students' copies, the number and specificity of the new scientific maxims could no longer be accommodated in this manner.

"Every author of new reading textbooks furnished generous instructions for the use of his materials. Furthermore, authors of texts which had appeared during the preceding period without detailed instructions now came forth with manuals....to furnish rather definitely prescribed instructions" (Smith, 1965, p. 169).

This explicit act to redirect teachers' interactions with students through the medium of a scientific teachers' manual is the beginning of basal reading materials—a technology true to its time, as each component found its roots in business, science, or psychology.

The logic of a teachers' manual makes perfect sense within the context of this time. First and foremost, the manual was an expression of the faith in the powers of science to discover the natural laws of reading and instruction. Not only were its originating maxims the results of scientific investigations but its entire rationale was founded on the idea that science should direct practice, that universal principles were preferable to the idiosyncratic behaviors of particular teachers and students. The directions to teachers, then, were offered as facts to be followed regardless of the social context of the instruction or the abilities and attitudes of children or teachers. These directions and materials would teach all children to read. This general tone of scientific authority was important to the eventual acceptance of the teachers' manuals because their directions did in fact require teachers to change their typical procedures, and few teachers were eager to alter procedures that had seemed successful in the past (Cuban, 1984). But who could argue with scientific facts?

The manuals also incorporated principles from business. After all, the manuals were an explicit attempt to standardize teachers' practice according to methods found to be most productive and economical. And why shouldn't scientific management work for education? It had been successful in business for over a decade. In a direct way the manuals solidified the bureaucratization of reading instruction. The manual separated the planning of instruction from the practice of instruction, and

This explicit act to redirect teachers' interactions with students through the medium of a scientific teachers' manual is the beginning of basal reading materials.

The teachers' manual contributed to the formalization of roles and rules for the business of teaching reading.

it provided "objective" criteria for judging the adequacy of a teacher's performance and the quality of the product, the students' performance. Both of these effects required a distinction to be made between the roles of teachers and administrators. Although the teacher remained the worker at the "chalk-face," the primary instructor, someone at a higher level of authority had to select the instructional goals and plans from among the many sets of basal materials available, and someone had to insure that teachers followed those selected plans. Thus, the teachers' manual contributed to the formalization of roles and rules for the business of teaching reading.

If we look at the crisis in reading instruction as a problem of bringing about more scientific, and thus more effective reading instruction from classroom teachers, as the reading experts of this time apparently did, then it is easy to understand the teachers' manual as a direct application of Thorndyke's psychology. The manual was the correct stimulus that would evoke the appropriate response from teachers. Teachers' subsequent reward for making this desired connection would come from the satisfaction in seeing their students learn to read faster and better, from their higher scores on tests, and in experiencing less pressure from administrators and the public.

In fact, Thorndyke's laws of learning became the basis for all the components of basal materials. For example, the *Law of Readiness* is demonstrated in the sequencing of skill instruction which is to prepare students for subsequent learning. The *Law of Exercise*—practice increases the strength of a connection—and silent reading techniques led to the invention of formal seatwork materials, workbooks and flashcards (Smith, 1965). Students' satisfaction from participating in basal-directed reading instruction (the *Law of Effect*) was to come from being able to read the literary and expository selection in the anthologies. Finally, the *Law of Identical Elements*—single connections should be tested in isolation—was first fulfilled by directions to analyze seatwork carefully and much later by the development of criterion and objective referenced tests which today accompany all sets of basal reading materials.

In summary, basal reading materials met the expectations of a public and profession enthralled with business, science, and psychology as they tried to find a remedy for the apparent crisis in reading instruction in schools and for the literacy of society. Moreover, basal materials appeared to be cost effective and thus worth the modest tax expenditure; they effectively bolstered weak supervision, and informed a poorly educated teaching staff. Promoted as the result of scientific study, basal materials promised that all children would learn to read well if teachers and students would simply follow the directions supplied in teachers' manuals. And although the contents of those directions would change from time to time during the next sixty years or so, the rationale for and the format of basal reading materials were set by the spirit of the first two decades of the twentieth century.

The rationale for and the format of basal reading materials were set by the spirit of the first two decades of the twentieth century.

GROWTH OF BASAL READING MATERIALS

Although there had long been professional educational experts such as Horace Mann, William Torrey Harris, and Francis Parker, these authorities were concerned with improving education as a whole. With the interest in the scientific investigation of education in the early twentieth century came a consequent division of education into areas of specialization. Perhaps foremost among these specialties was the scientific study of reading, which quickly spawned the reading expert steeped in facts and figures and intent on discovering the laws of reading. Many of these experts believed that understanding reading was the key to unlocking the secrets of the mind in general.

Edmund Burke Huey (1908-1968) offered a challenge to this new group: "After all we have thus far been content with trial and error, too often allowing publishers to be our jury, and a real rationalization of the process of inducing the child with the practice of reading has not been made" (p. 9). For Huey and many others instructional materials appeared to be a roadblock. But by 1928 basal materials seemed to be the technology through which the experts would introduce scientific reading instruction to the public schools:

> In these places we find teachers instructing children as they themselves were taught, absolutely ignorant and oblivious that science had discovered for us truths and that little children are entitled to the benefits of these discoveries.....One of the most potent factors in spreading of the results of research is through a well prepared set of readers and their manuals (Donovan, 1928, p. 106-07).

With very few exceptions early reading experts supported teachers' use of basal materials through most of the media available to them. First, professional books of these and later times implied or stated explicitly that carefully following the directions in teachers' manuals would teach students to read. For example, in *Silent and Oral Reading: A Practical Handbook of Methods Based on the Most Recent Scientific Investigation*, Stone (1922) argued that "the best practice will involve the use of all three primers during the first few months of instruction" (p. 45).

Durrell (1940) was more emphatic:

> The advantage of orderly procedures in reading instruction is such that few, if any, teachers can serve all pupils well by incidental or improvised reading methods...the well planned basal reading systems presented by experienced textbook publishers have many advantages....A detailed study of the manuals of basal reading systems is the first step to learning how to teach reading (p. 22).

Dolch (1950) added:

> A basic reader is really one part of a system for

teaching reading. This system includes the basic books themselves, the workbooks that go with them, and the teachers' manual, which tells what to do with the text-books, what to do with the workbooks, and also tells all the other activities a teacher should go through in order to do a complete job of teaching reading (p. 319).

Another means the reading experts used to voice their support for basal materials was the *NSSE Year-book*. In the *Twenty-Fourth Yearbook* (Gray, 1925), the Committee on Reading was careful not to recommend one set of basal materials over another because "to se-lect from among these materials would require an amount of scientific data which the Committee does not possess" (p. 173). However, they did establish stan-dards for basal reading materials based on the recom-mendations of Ernest Horn. In the *Thirty-Sixth Yearbook* (Gray, 1937), William S. Gray was clear:

Furthermore, prepared materials are, as a rule, more skillfully organized and are technically superior to those developed daily in classrooms. Because they fol-low a sequential plan, the chance for so called "gaps" in learning is greatly reduced (p. 90-91).

With a Committee on Reading composed entirely of basal authors, the *Forty-Eighth Yearbook* (Gates, 1949) suggested:

Improvements in the construction and use of reading materials have contributed appreciatively to the im-provement of primary reading instruction (p. 56)…it should be remembered that, as a rule, pupils gain most from the use of a reader when the selections contained in that book are taught as the authors of the reader in-tend them to be taught (p. 131).

… the teacher who attempts to prepare substitutes for basic readers…ought to make the substitutes better than the readers…available (p. 152).

And, after forty years of basal readers, in *Innovation and Change in Reading Instruction*, the *Sixty-Seventh Year-book* (Robinson, 1968), the Committee acknowledged

*Most of the lead-
ing reading experts
were under con-
tract to basal pub-
lishing companies.*

that one thing would not change—"basal readers will
continue to be used..." (p. 124).

Publishers of basal reading materials managed to
maintain the appearance of keeping pace with the
rapid expansion of scientific information in the increas-
ingly more frequently revised editions of their publications. That is, as new skills, periods of development,
and theories were discovered, basal publishers could
claim their revisions supplied additional information
and materials to help teachers follow scientific developments. This parallel in development is understandable since most of the leading reading experts were
under contract to basal publishing companies: Ernest
Horn, Arthur Gates, and Gray in the 1920s and 1930s;
Emmett Betts, David Russell, and Paul McKee in the
1940s and 50s; Guy Bond, Albert Harris, and Russell
Stauffer in the 1960s; Kenneth Goodman, P. David
Pearson, and Robert Ruddell in the 1970s and Richard
Allington, Donna Alvermann, and Robert Tierney in
the 1980s. Readiness materials, separate teachers' manuals for each grade level, and controlled vocabularies
are but a few of the modifications that were made and
continue to the present.

All of this growth in the market, and therefore the
profitability of these materials, did not go unnoticed by
large communication companies—Xerox, RCA, IBM,
CBS, and others came in and then out of basal publishing by buying and then selling educational publishing
houses.

As anyone even remotely associated with elementary-school reading instruction knows, the number of
components which comprise basal materials has grown
dramatically over the decades. Not only have the readers become more realistic and colorful, the teachers'
manuals more explicit and elaborate, and the seatwork
more plentiful and varied but new components have
been added to the "basal reading system." Although
new, these components fit well within the parameters
set by Thorndyke's Laws of Learning which informed

the rationale for basals at their inception. For example, charts were published to standardize the stimuli for each skill in order to evoke the appropriate student response and to relieve teachers from repetitive boardwork; objective- and criterion-referenced tests were introduced which matched the basal lessons in order to meet the *Law of Identical Elements* (isolated skill testing) more adequately and to ensure objectively that students were ready for the next skill; and management systems were established to enable parents, administrators, and teachers to follow students' progress through the basal's scope and sequence of skills. After an examination of all major sets of basals, the Educational Products Information Exchange (1977) concluded that these sets were more alike than different and that those few exceptions were rarely used in elementary classrooms.

... many individuals could not tell one (basal) program from another when they examined instructional materials (Farr, Tulley & Powell, 1987, p. 268).

> Indeed, in some of our interviews with textbook adoption committee members, many individuals could not tell one (basal) program from another when they examined instructional materials without seeing the name of the program, even though these interviews took place immediately after the committee members had completed a several month review of the materials and had selected the program that they believed was best for their school or district (Farr, Tulley & Powell, 1987, p. 268).

To be sure, not all reading experts were in favor of the growing influence of basal materials in elementary reading instruction. Germane and Germane (1922) found that "unfortunately too many teachers used only one book—the regular school reader" (p. 92). Boney (1938, 1939) criticized the *NSSE Thirty-Six Yearbook's* unqualified endorsement of teachers' use of basal materials citing high test scores from districts which did not use basals. In the thirtieth anniversary issue of *Elementary English*, Dolch (1954) reversed his earlier endorsement and railed against attempts to produce "teacher-proof" materials; and one year later, Rudolph Flesch (1955) blamed poorly designed basal materials

"The teachers believe that the suggestions to teachers found in reading manuals are based on 'definite scientific proof': almost no teacher disagrees."

for *Why Johnny Can't Read*. Jeanne Chall (1967) conducted a four-year evaluation of the components, contents, and use of basal materials and concluded that the materials were a product of convention not science. In a series of studies Dolores Durkin (1974, 1975, 1978-79, 1981) attempted to modify teachers' "slavish" adherence to the directions in teachers' manuals and unthoughtful use of seatwork. And throughout the growth of basal materials, advocates of the (not so) New Education and later whole language philosophy conducted a running battle in educational journals against basal materials and their detrimental effects on students' desire and ability to learn to read (Moore, 1985; Goodman, 1979, 1986).

Despite these frequent, but peripheral, objections, the use of basal materials was almost universal in American schools by the 1960s. In the *Columbia-Carnegie Study of Reading Research and Its Communication*, Barton and Wilder (1964) found that over 90 percent of the teachers from the 300 schools that they surveyed used basal materials on "all or most days in the year" (p. 362). Moreover, the association of basal materials with scientific instruction was virtually complete: "The teachers believe that the suggestions to teachers found in reading manuals are based on 'definite scientific proof': almost no teacher disagrees" (p. 382). In the *Harvard Report on Reading in Elementary Schools*, "It became apparent from observation by the study staff in classrooms and from interviews with school personnel that far too many teachers follow the [teachers'] manual literally, seldom if ever exercising their own initiative and creativity in teaching reading" (Austin & Morrison, 1963, p. 223). Contrary to the recommendations of these reports, the percentage of teachers relying on basal materials increased to 94 percent in a survey of 10,000 elementary teachers in the 1970s (Educational Products Information Exchange, 1977).

In the conclusion to their study Barton and Wilder

(1964) pointed out the paradox for elementary-school teachers in continuing this practice:

> Teachers think they are professional—but want to rely on basal readers, graded workbooks, teachers' manuals, and other materials prefabricated by the experts (p. 382).

3

THE STATUS OF BASAL READING MATERIALS

Barton and Wilder's (1964) comment suggests that although teachers want to think of themselves as professionals, their heavy reliance on basal reading materials makes observers of their work skeptical of that professionalism. Professionals control their work and make critical judgments about what procedures and materials are most suitable for specific situations (Lortie, 1975). Yet few teachers appear to be moving away from the major obstacle to their attainment of that status during reading instruction; that is, away from slavish reliance on basal reading materials. To understand this paradox we must look at the factors which contribute to teachers' apparent reluctance: objective factors, those beyond teachers' control like expert opinion, state intervention, district administrative policy, and publishers' marketing, as well as subjective factors, those within their control such as their involvement with their work and their beliefs about reading, instruction, and materials.

OBJECTIVE FACTORS

Expert Opinion

Because basal use is now so pervasive, discussions of teacher professionalism during reading instruction most often center on *how* teachers use basals. Even though teachers are now college educated the question is: Should teachers follow the directions in teachers' manuals closely (technical use) or should they decide which of those directions are pertinent to their situation (substantive use)? Though many reading experts support the substantive position, they still reinforce the idea that teachers should rely on basal materials because they consistently begin their discussions with the assumption that teachers will not use alternatives to basal materials when teaching reading and therefore, these experts confine their discussions to choosing among options within the basal format.

Few experts venture beyond basal-directed instruction, it seems, because they believe that discussions of alternative ways of conducting reading instruction are irrelevant for America. Even many vocal critics end up supporting their use. This emphasis is demonstrated in recent methods textbooks, research on teacher decision making and contents of basal materials, and the most recent report on the state of American reading instruction, *Becoming a Nation of Readers* (Commission on Reading, 1985).

Most reading methods textbooks offer three reasons for their relatively unqualified support of teachers' reliance on materials:

1. The reading selections are of high quality.
2. Teachers' manuals offer suggestions for comprehensive and systematic instruction.
3. The materials are based on scientific investigations of the reading process (Shannon, 1983a).

Although textbook authors occasionally warn teachers against the mechanical use of the manual, the depth of the textbook authors commitment to basal-directed reading instruction is shown in their allotment of page space and the language they use in their explanation of the basal components. In a random sample of six methods textbooks (from a population of thirty), authors devoted between eleven and thirty-six pages with between six and nineteen accompanying reproductions to their description of basal materials, yet they allotted between zero and one and a half pages to discussions of finding the main idea of a passage. Moreover, five of the six textbooks included terms like "best routines," "developed by teams of reading experts," and "objective tightly structured and logically ordered" in rationales as to why basals should be used. Only one author provided specific suggestions concerning how teachers might become substantive in their use of basals.

Perhaps the most extreme example of methods textbook support for teachers' use of basals is Robert Aukerman's *The Basal Reader Approach to Reading* (1981), in which he describes the fifteen leading sets of basal reading materials for 333 pages.

In a summary of studies concerning teacher decision making during reading instruction Duffy and Ball (1986) conclude:

> ...the data suggest that teachers do not rely upon rational models to make decisions about developing students' understanding, but instead, focus on procedural concerns regarding classroom organization and management ... which encourage teachers to follow the prescriptions of the instructional materials in a technical rather than a professional manner..." (p. 173).

Attempts to help teachers become substantive in their use of basals yielded short-lived results because "neither the content nor the instructional design offered much structure for decision making" (Duffy, Roehler, & Putnam, 1987, p. 360), and it took too much time and effort for teachers to render basal materials substantively useful. Yet Duffy, Roehler, and Putnam concluded that "the solution does not lie with abandoning basal textbooks" because "all teachers appreciate the guide" (p. 362).

"Neither the content nor the instructional design offered much structure for decision making" (Duffy, Roehler, & Putnam).

Other researchers study teachers' professionalism within this narrow focus by comparing teachers' instructional actions against the directions offered in teachers' manuals. Shake and Allington (1985) found that when second-grade teachers were selective about basal directions they often offered poor substitutes for the recommended questions after a story. Barr (1986) extended this type of research to include before, during, and after basal story activities and found that "teachers do engage in active decision making to determine which of the recommended activities should be incorporated into prereading instruction" (p. 13), although "suggestions in the guides are systematically reflected in prereading activities" (p. 18). She concludes her study where it began with the assumption that "basal programs form the backbone of instruction" (p. 18) and that teachers should be taught to be substantive in their use of them.

Perhaps the most time-honored support for teachers' continued reliance on basal materials comes from attempts to influence classroom reading instruction through the alteration of basal materials:

> Common experience, as well as systematic classroom observation, indicates that published basal readers and content area texts have an enormous, even overriding influence on how reading, social studies, and science are taught in the nation's schools. It stands to reason, therefore, that researchers who wish to have scholarship influence practice ought to give a high priority to interacting with publishers...(Anderson, Osborn & Tierney, 1984, p. ix).

This effort, spearheaded by the Center for the Study of Reading at the University of Illinois, found basal readers (Bruce, 1984), teachers' manuals (Beck, 1984; Durkin, 1984), and workbooks (Osborn, 1984) all wanting and as a result responsible for poor instruction. Although the authors mention teachers in their discussions, few entertain the possibility that teachers abandon all or parts of the basal materials that they find objectionable. Rather, they summarize their results for policymakers (Osborn, Wilson & Anderson, 1985) and for publishers (Tierney, 1984a) in order to evoke change. Only after being told by publishers that they would not alter their materials unless there was an existing market for them did the Center accept the "challenge...to communicate current reading research (as well as exemplars of good practice) to a designated group of people: teachers, administrators, and other members of textbook adoption committees" (Dole, Rogers & Osborn, 1987, p. 284) through a series of booklets, *A Guide to Selecting Basal Reading Programs.*

Much of *Becoming a Nation of Readers (Commission on Reading, 1985)* is devoted to a discussion of basal materials and their use. This is understandable given their charge from the National Academy of Education to report on American reading instruction. However, at times the Committee seems to apologize for this attention: "In most classrooms, the instruction will be driven by a basal reading program. For this reason, the importance of these programs cannot be underestimated and will be briefly discussed here" (p. 34). The implication is that the Committee only discusses basal materials because teachers rely on them; yet their firm commitment to these materials is found in their discussion of "Whole Language" approaches to teaching reading. First, they acknowledge that these methods have been used successfully in New Zealand, "the most literate country in the world," and that "in the hands of very skillful [American] teachers, the results can be excellent" (p. 45). However, citing *First Grade Studies* (Bond & Dykstra, 1967) as evidence, they argue "but average results are indifferent when compared to approaches typical in American classrooms" (p. 45). Since the Committee had already stated that most American teachers use basal materials they leave little doubt about which method they recommend. Moreover, they leave entirely unexamined the reasons why this alternative to basal materials has been successful in New Zealand or why New Zealand teachers seem

"In most classrooms, the instruction will be driven by a basal reading program."

Many of those who appear to be calling for change in basals have their names on basals as authors.

to be very skillful in comparison to average American teachers.

What is most disturbing in all these examples of current reading experts' support for teachers' use of basals is the confusion caused by the contradiction between their criticism and their recommendations. While all convey that teachers should be professionals in the teaching of reading, the experts narrow the parameters of that professionalism to choosing among alternatives within the basal framework and/or being more knowledgeable about how to use the basals best. Indeed these experts make the real decision—which approach to use—before they begin to include teachers in their discussions. Teachers are left only with quasi-decisions of selecting how much of which basal parts to use.

Thus, when teachers read most methods textbooks, peruse reading journals or professional books, or attend reading conferences, they find reading experts supporting the use of basal reading materials. And many of those who appear to be calling for change in basals have their names on basals as authors.

State Intervention

In southern, southwestern, and most western states the most obvious connection between the government and reading instruction is the state level committee that chooses which ones among all basal series on the market local districts must choose if they wish state funding for textbook purchases.

Three rationales are often given for this centralized adoption policy:

1. a reduction in textbook cost through volume purchase
2. the selection of better textbooks
3. some assurance of a uniform statewide curriculum (Tulley, 1983).

While this policy has obvious effects on the reading

instruction in adoption states, it also influences the reading instruction in non-adoption states through a phenomenon called the "California" or "Texas" effect. These states and large urban districts influence the date and contents of basal revisions (Squire, 1985). For example, basal reader "birthday parties are devoid of ice cream and cake (California considers them junk food), while many adventures occur with Texas backdrops. (Texas, which dominates control of the market with its unique direct purchase of textbooks, prefers Texas settings)" (Muther, 1985, p.7).

Perhaps of greater importance is the considerable influence on basals' structure and goals of these states because publishers attempt to align their products with the curriculum outlines and instructional guidelines from Texas' and California's departments of education (Follett, 1985).

While state adoptions almost preclude teachers from using other materials as the basis for reading instruction—few districts are willing to forego state textbook funds—the state affects reading instruction in other ways also. For example Texas teachers are subject to a fifty dollar fine if they are caught teaching reading without an approved textbook. Although this may be an extreme example, most state legislatures have recently taken a more active role in elementary education (Darling-Hammond & Wise, 1985). Certainly politicians have always been concerned about schooling—Joseph Mayer Rice considered it one major reason for poor, mechanical teaching in 1893—but this previous intervention was different in scope and intent. The new state initiatives attempt to standardize the goals of schooling as basic skills, to set time limits for elementary school subjects, and to regulate textbook content (Wise, 1979). Regardless of their intention, these laws have restrictive effects on reading programs. For example, Florida's Educational Accountability Act of 1976 required "effective, meaningful, and relevant educational experience designed to give students at least the minimum skills necessary to function and survive in today's society" (as quoted in Wise, 1979, p. 25), and because meaningful and relevant experiences were difficult to monitor the legislature settled for minimum competence examinations to determine instructional effectiveness among districts.

The method to meet these minimum goals was not left to school district or teachers' discretion when Florida passed a law which required "written proof of the use of the learner-verification and revision process during preparation, development, and post publication revision of the materials...themselves, revision of the teachers' materials, and revision of the teachers' skill through retraining..." (as quoted in Wise, 1979, p. 22-23). The intent was to promote better materials, but in effect this law set up basal materials as the only legal means for providing reading instruction, and it set up basal publishers as the instructional monitors of teachers' instruction. All told, Florida legislated basic skills as the goals of reading instruction, basal materials as the means of reading instruction, and minimal competency tests and basal publishers as the monitor of program effectiveness. In short, the laws required the technological management of reading instruction in Florida.

Government, then, not only makes basals available cheaply but it also sets limits on how, when, and for what purpose the basals will be used. Even many of the twenty-eight nonadoption states have minimum competence tests and time requirements for each subject. As a result of this legislated learning a formal system of accountability is established which makes the school district more responsible to the state than it is responsive to its public (Frymier, 1985). This pressure on districts to meet standard goals, means, and time is in turn translated by district administrators into expectations for standard performance from individual teachers.

District Administrative Policy

In virtually all school districts a textbook adoption committee is convened periodically to select one, or less often more than one, set of basal materials to be used in district elementary schools for the following several years. This practice is found in adoption states as districts pick from an authorized list and in non-adoption states as districts deal directly with fifteen to eighteen basal publishers. In most cases "the selection of a basal reader is tantamount to selecting the reading curriculum" (Farr, Tulley & Powell, 1987, p. 268), as the basal's scope and sequence of skills determines the goals for the district, the teachers' manuals become the instructional outlines, the pupils' readers the reading materials, the workbooks and worksheets the practice activities, and the criterion-referenced tests the means for the evaluation of student progress.

Despite the obvious importance of the committee's decision, most studies are not very laudatory in their description of adoption committee operations (see Farr, Tulley & Powell, 1987 for a review of this research). They suggest that little time is devoted to the actual examination of basal materials, that committee members work from checklists which emphasize the presence of aspects rather than an evaluation of their quality, that committee members are often unduly influenced by publishing company representatives, and that few classroom teachers are directly involved in the selection process. The results, by all accounts, is a basal program selected more for its surface appearance and its representation than for its underlying philosophy or instructional design.

Unfortunately, attempts to help committees make more rational decisions have met with mixed results (Dole, Rogers, & Osborn, 1987). That is partly because these efforts have focussed on getting the committees to choose materials that are most consistent in their technology and have not focussed on how committees can spell out specifications for what the district's pro-

"The selection of a basal reader is tantamount to selecting the reading curriculum" (Farr, Tulley & Powell).

Most studies are not very laudatory in their description of adoption committee operations (Farr, Tulley & Powell).

fessionals want in the way of materials before judging what's available by these professional criteria.

Regardless of how basal materials are selected, once they are in place they become the focus of district accountability systems which are established to insure that state standards are met. Most often these systems are organized around straight-forward administrative directives concerning how the basal materials should be used (Duffy, Roehler & Wesselman, 1985). At times, they are accompanied by schedules for expected basal coverage (Shannon, 1986a). Often tests, which accompany the basals, serve to monitor teachers' adherence to the schedule or implementation of the directives (Shannon, 1983b). Because these tests are geared to the parent basal (Johnson & Pearson, 1975), administrators can keep track of teachers' and students' use of basal materials without intrusive observation. However, some districts opt for direct observation with observation checklists based on the results of school and teacher effectiveness research (Cuban, 1984; Ramsey, 1987). At least one district tied their directives for basal use to the state's minimum competence examination, offering merit pay rewards for schools that meet growth quotas set by central administrators (Shannon, 1986b).

In each of these systems the result is usually the same. Teachers feel pressured to follow the directions in teachers' manuals closely and reject alternative ways to teach reading as threats to their job security (Duffy, Roehler, & Putnam, 1987; Shannon, 1987). In sum, they let the basal publishers decide how to teach students to read.

Publishers' Marketing

Like all businesses in a capitalist economy, basal publishers must compete with one another to acquire a segment of the markets. They do this by reacting to, conserving, and creating their market. Perhaps, the publishing industry's most successful reaction to its market was its original promise that basal materials constitute a complete and indispensible technology through which scientific reading instruction can be conducted. This promise continues to influence state legislators, textbook adoption committees, and other school personnel; and it well may be at the root of the problem concerning the superficial evaluation of basal materials during textbook adoption—committee members presume all basals to be scientifically sound. When committees find basals to be so similar in content and design they take that as confirmation of the scientific basis of basal materials.

"Publishers are dependent on sales for survival." (Follett)

If the surface level is of greatest importance to the adoption committees then it is of equal importance to publishers who view "the textbook adoption process as the system that produces sales. Publishers are dependent on sales for survival" (Follett, 1985, p. 19). Publishers put nearly equal amounts in their budgets for research and development and for marketing. *Becoming a Nation of Readers* estimates $15,000,000 as the average cost for each edition of a basal series; Graham's estimate in the mid-70's was $20,000,000 (Graham, 1978). More recent estimates are for costs at over $35 million dollars (Squire, 1987). This is not an inconsequential sum. The marketing budget is used to attract textbook committee members' attention to the publisher's products. Publishers rely on:

> ...influential marketing strategies [which] include providing free items that the district might not otherwise purchase, hosting dinners or wine and cheese receptions, trying to influence key people and providing in-service sessions for added exposure to the company. Some companies host summer institutes for extended exposure for their companies and textbook programs to which key school personnel are invited, with all expenses paid (Farr, Tulley & Powell, 1987, p. 275).

Once successful, publishers attempt to conserve their percentage of the market while attracting new customers by incorporating whatever educational rhetoric seems popular at the time while refraining from mak-

ing any substantial changes. Durkin (1987) demonstrates how teachers' manuals adopted only the spirit
of the 1960s by featuring the terminology of phonics
while maintaining the status quo concerning "decoding" instruction, the spirit of the 1970s by creating basal
management systems to deflect the competition from
nonbasal management systems, and the spirit of the
1980s by highlighting the correlations between the
basal goals and those of standardized achievement
tests. While the marketing strategies and terminology
changed for the new customers, the program remained
essentially the same to keep previous customers
satisfied.

American publishers have never seemed attracted to
the notion of offering alternative instructional packages
to meet the needs of teachers with differing instructional philosophies. That has left a small but profitable vac-
uum for such companies as Scholastic, on the one
hand, which offers kits centered around Trade books,
and Economy, on the other, which offers programs that
focus more explicitly on phonics. Holt, Rinehart and
Winston, using the talents of Bill Martin Jr., published
innovative literature based materials but they were always offered as supplemental and not as an alternative
to the basals.

Few businesses would survive if they simply reacted
to or conserved their markets; they must create new
markets for their product or increase demand for additional products within the current market. Rather than
offering alternate products, basal publishers have created new required or optional equipment, workbooks,
worksheets, charts, kits, special paper, flash cards, etc.
Most of these materials are consumed by students each
year and must be repurchased before the start of the
next school year. Although each product can be
justified according to Thorndyke's Laws of Learning,
the bottom line, so to speak, is that they generate
profits for publishing companies and go a long way to
recouping the millions spent on each edition. Teachers

seem to have insatiable appetites for these consumable products (Follett, 1985).

American publishers have attempted to find foreign markets either by direct export of American basals or by creating adapted editions through subsidiaries in other English speaking countries. They have not been particularly successful. One reason may be the rejection by teachers in these other countries of the thick directive manuals. Reading schemes in these countries have had only minimal manuals for their use.

McInnis describes how Canadian publishers have been dismantling basals since Canadian schools ended their reliance on American basals in 1962 and began to produce their own:

> We had to dismantle the use of readability formulas. They disappeared very early in the sixties.... One of the first things we dismantled in 1960 was end of level tests....We had to reduce the training focus—the training on the ... parts of words....Word lists were discontinued. This was a terrible struggle because teachers kept writing in for the word lists.... This dismantling has had to go on ... it has to come, first of all from pressure from the field, from teachers who will say "We don't want that; it interferes with our work" (McInnis, 1987).

More recently, there has been a movement among American publishers to export the basal technology to Spanish language reading instruction in order to serve a growing market within the United States. In some instances these are virtually verbatim translations of the English-language basals (Freeman, 1987).

In summary, these objective factors—expert opinion, state intervention, administrative policy, and publishers' marketing—comprise the constraints on teachers' options during reading instruction. Each in its own way contributes to teachers' reliance on basal materials as it reinforces the notion that following the directions in teachers' manuals is safe, scientific, lawful, expected, and pleasant.

Canadian publishers have been dismantling basals since Canadian schools ended their reliance on American basals in 1962.

SUBJECTIVE FACTORS

It would be a mistake to conclude that objective factors force teachers to reject professionalism during reading instruction and use basals in a technical manner. Teachers' reliance on basal materials is not that simple, and the truth is that most teachers seem reasonably content with their reading instruction. Admittedly, teachers complain about some particulars of their reading programs and react negatively to the single-mindedness of some of the "objective" factors (Shannon, 1986b). But overall they seem satisfied with the time-saving benefits and the results that basal materials seem to offer. Only recently, in the whole language movement, have we seen a substantial upsurge in overt resistance to basal use. And that has only come after huge grass-roots movements in New Zealand, Australia, England, and, particularly, Canada.

No one or two factors could impose such strict compliance on over 90 percent of any group who are spread across the country and are allowed to teach behind closed doors; that is, unless the group agreed with the practice in some way. Objective factors are real and pervasive, but most teachers seem to go along with the technical use of basals even though it works against their professional status to do so. Why do so many teachers give up their decision making to the basals? We believe the answer lies in teachers' internalization of the rhetoric that has surrounded basal materials from the beginning.

In an investigation of why teachers rely so heavily on basal materials Shannon (1983b) found that 445 teachers from one school district believed foremost that they were fulfilling administrative expectations when they used basal materials. Many listed unequal representation on basal adoption committees, explicit directives to use one set of basals exclusively, and a criterion-referenced test accountability system as evidence to support their opinions. When interviewed, administrators justified their expectations for the use of basals on the notion that the materials can teach students to read because the materials are based on scientific investigations of the reading process. At first glance objective factors do indeed seem to determine teachers' instructional behaviors. Yet when teachers were asked what they would do differently if administrators did not require basal use, 84 percent of them offered the same rationales as administrators for their continued reliance on basal materials, with one slight deviation—teachers would include more alternate sets of basal materials in order to meet students' needs while remaining within the parameters of the original curriculum. These results and those of several follow-up studies (Shannon, 1984, 1986a, 1986b, 1986c) suggest that teachers have internalized the basic promise made by basal materials.

84 percent of them offered the same rationales as administrators for their continued reliance on basal materials.

Acceptance of the instructional powers and the scientific validity of basals leads teachers to separate themselves from what might be considered responsibility for the totality of reading instruction (Purves, 1984). That is, rather than consider the long range goals for their school's reading program, they let the basals set those goals. Rather than puzzle over the logic of the skills sequence at their grade level, they push ahead because "you can't understand it, you can only follow it" (Duffy, Roehler, & Putnam, 1987, P. 362). Rather than outline daily objectives, they read them from the teachers' manual. In Shannon's study (1983b) fewer than 7 percent of the 445 teachers objected to the separation of planning goals from the process of teaching. These acts are not willful neglect of their jobs—"it's just the way it is." It's the way they define their work. To these teachers reading instruction appears as an exchange between *things:* basal materials that have the power to instruct and students who can absorb that instruction. They see their jobs as teachers to be that of insuring students progress through the basals. So they are like technicians keeping an industrial production line moving.

Even when they do experience a problem with the materials most often teachers close their classroom doors and "make do."

In this exchange between *things,* teachers may lose sight of the fact that reading instruction is a human process—a collaboration among authors, teachers and students—and may stop trying to make human sense out of their work. Rather, they defer to the basal materials as the technological solution to the problem of teaching all students to read according to scientific principles. In a very real sense teachers' knowledge of reading and instruction becomes frozen in this single technological form. They treat reading instruction as the application of these materials and believe that this act fulfills their instructional responsibilities (Duffy & McIntyre, 1980). Ultimately, teachers, like administrators and basal authors, define their successes during reading instruction in terms of the efficiency of their delivery of basal lessons and students' gains on basal and standardized tests.

Within this basal logic, teachers act rationally in all activities related to reading instruction. Not only do they follow the directions in the teachers' manuals during reading instruction (Barr, 1986) but they cover all the skills and use all the worksheets because the skills will appear on the basal tests using the same format and vocabulary as the worksheets (Shannon, 1983b). Teachers seek practical ways in which to improve their use of basals when they attend reading methods classes or read professional journals, and often seem uninterested in esoteric discussions of theory because they find reading theory in their teachers' manuals. At reading conferences they peruse the book exhibits hoping to find additional materials to solve their instructional problems and gratefully accept the free samples that publishers offer. Teachers participate in schemes to raise achievement test scores by practice testing and teaching to the test because "that's how everyone defines our success" (Shannon, 1986b). Even when they do experience a problem with the materials most often teachers close their classroom doors and "make do."

Each of these acts demonstrates that the majority of

teachers are actively involved in their reliance on basal materials, they do not simply acquiesce to the pressures of objective factors. Despite college educations (or perhaps because of that education), the rhetoric from the 1920s concerning the Laws of Learning, the principles of business, and the power of science still seem to find an accepting audience among teachers and other school personnel for that matter (Shannon, 1987). A dramatic example of this is found in a claimed 65 percent drop in sales experienced by Scott, Foresman and Company when they published a basal series which, among other deviations, encourages teachers to act professionally and to make judgments about the goals and objectives to fit the needs of particular students (Tierney, 1984b).

In the end teachers' technical use of the basal is not the result of teachers behaving irrationally during their reading instruction periods, as many critics claim, rather teachers act all too rationally as they work within the promise of the basal program.

4

THE ECONOMICS OF BASAL READERS

While schools have accepted the concept that business methods can be applied to the teaching of reading, business has taken the basal to its heart. Education itself is big business. It generates 6.5 percent of the Gross National Product, a total of around $260 billion (McGraw, 1984). Of that amount, around $1.5 billion is spent on books at all levels of education.

Just how that amount is distributed by educational level, by subject, and by particular publisher is something of an industrial secret. In fact, the more specific the information sought, such as the gross and net sales of a particular basal series in a particular year, the more closely the information is guarded. Annual reports to stockholders give only composite and general figures. Dollars spent on educational books is reported by *Publishers Weekly*, which gives figures for the combined overall totals for elementary and secondary school textbooks. These figures are not broken down to show money spent on specific types of educational publications. With the exception of *Book Publishing Annual*,

About 80 percent of the money spent on basals goes for the top six programs.

which has a section on school publishing, there is little easily accessible information about the economic specifics of the school-book industry. Most of what we report here comes from these sources and personal communication from the Association of American Publishers (AAP).

The AAP reported that $1.481 billion was spent in 1985 on textbooks in the United States for kindergarten through twelfth grade. Of that figure, $872 million was spent on elementary-school textbooks. It is estimated that 35-40 percent of that amount was spent on basal readers, roughly one-third of a billion dollars. This proportion of spending on basal readers seems more stable than for other subjects, which tend to fluctuate from year to year. It is not uncommon for school systems or states to adopt new basals every five years. A fair proportion of the total for the basals goes for consumable materials, such as workbooks which must be replaced every year. These consumables contribute considerably to the profitability of the basal program.

About 80 percent of the money spent on basals goes for the top six programs (in the mid-1980s) listed below alphabetically rather than by sales or profits:

> Ginn and Company (now Silver Burdett and Ginn, which is a subsidiary of Simon and Schuster publishing group, publishing division of Gulf and Western. Allyn and Bacon and Curriculum Concepts, which also publish reading programs, are owned by the Simon and Schuster subsidiary)
> Harcourt, Brace and Jovanovich
> Holt, Rinehart and Winston (recently purchased from CBS by Harcourt)
> Houghton Mifflin (which also owns Riverside)
> Macmillan (which now owns Harper and Row, Lippincott, and Laidlaw—all marketed under Scribner Education).
> Scott, Foresman (recently acquired by Time-Life)

Graham reports that a 1977 study by Market Data Retrieval showed the same six publishers plus Harper and Row (ranked fourth that year; its school department now owned by Macmillan), as the top seven publishers in sales (Graham, 1978). D.C. Heath has acquired American Book Company. McGraw-Hill now owns Economy.

Ironically, the huge size of the basal market has not induced a great deal of diversity but rather has caused the major publishers to think of any basal program that has not achieved massive success as a failure. A few companies have offered second-line programs "for those pupils for whom learning to read isn't as easy as ABC," as Scott, Foresman puts it. But, in general, American publishers have put all their marketing efforts into single, heavily promoted basal offerings. Squire reports that in 1985 the average pre-tax profit of school publishers was 17.8 percent. But the largest publishers averaged 22.7 percent while small publishers, "essentially uneconomical in today's high cost markets," averaged only 6.6 percent (Squire, 1987). Independents find it hard to compete in raising capital to develop a program and in the expensive marketing campaigns of the decreasing number of publishing giants.

An earlier trend of publishers being absorbed by conglomerates has given way to buyouts and mergers, made possible by the current government's administration's relaxation of the antitrust laws. As a result publishers are absorbing each other, leading to larger market shares and fewer competing companies. The basal text publisher brings together two central trends in twentieth-century America: the technologizing of the school curriculum with the textbook becoming "an exemplar of technical form," and the industrialization and centralization of the publishing process. It's logical that basals would show this heightened trend with a very large capital investment, a concentration on mass markets, and with sales being not on a copy-by-copy basis but on huge adoptions that result in thousands of copies being sold over a period of years. As a result of recent mergers some leading companies are currently

Publishers are absorbing each other, leading to larger market shares and fewer competing companies.

marketing two or more programs. Whether they will continue to do so can't be determined at this time.

Profits for these companies fluctuate depending on timing of revisions, introduction of new series and state and local adoptions. Expenditures other than marketing are virtually all upfront, sometimes years before any sales are made. Publishers are reluctant to put a series on the market until the full program, K-6(or 8), and all its components are available, lest they risk being frozen out of adoptions. Publishers make frequent revisions in order to be able to go into adoption competitions with the most recent copyright dates.

The $300-400 million plus spent on basals compares to about $72 million spent in the same year on juvenile Trade hardback and softcover books. Of that, only about $3 million was spent on paperbacks. Though California is calling for increased use of Trade books in the classroom, the major portion of the Trade book expenditures is in school libraries. In many elementary schools that lack even rudimentary libraries there is virtually nothing for pupils to read except what is in the basal. Many states restrict or prohibit spending of state textbook funds for Trade books. Teachers who want to replace or supplement the basals in their classrooms with paperbacks often do so at their own expense.

MORAL ISSUES IN MAKING AND MARKETING BASALS

A riverboat leaves the levee near the French Quarter in New Orleans heading up the Mississippi for a moonlight cruise. Its passengers are teachers, reading specialists, school administrators and teacher educators attending the annual meeting of the International Reading Association (IRA), guests of a major publisher which has chartered the boat. Food, drink, and entertainment are provided by the publisher.

Another year. A publisher takes over the Franklin Institute in Philadelphia for a lavish evening of food, drink and entertainment for its guests who are attending the IRA conference. Down the street still another publisher is loading its guests, also conference attendees, on buses. They will be taken to Atlantic City for an evening's entertainment including gambling courtesy of their host, the publisher of a basal billed as a phonics program.

In a context in which the major products are hard to distinguish from each other, marketing advantages are crucial.

These lavish entertainments are part of the tradition of marketing the products of American industry. In school publishing single decisions made at state, local, and sometimes school levels can assure huge sales over an extended period or shut particular publishers out. In a context in which the major products are hard to distinguish from each other, marketing advantages are crucial. So publishers spend money both broadly and selectively to woo those who may influence the decisions. The intensity of this marketing competition creates the potential for conflicts of interest at many levels. It creates moral and potential legal problems. Consider these aspects:

1. National professional organizations depend on income from exhibitors at their conventions not only to make the conventions profitable but also to carry on the business of the organization. In one year IRA showed an excess of income over expenses at the annual meeting of $300,000. That was almost exactly equal to the income from exhibitors' fees. NCTE has customarily blocked periods of time at their conventions when no sessions are scheduled so those attending will be encouraged to visit the exhibits.

2. State and local meetings of professional organizations frequently rely on publishers to provide , at the publishers' expense, program speakers who are authors. Sales representatives will make the arrangements, pick up the speakers, and deliver them to the meetings. It would be an act of ingratitude for the program chair, who may also be the

chair of a local text selection committee, to deny the sale rep's request for an opportunity to pitch his/her wares before the committee. Text authors, furthermore, though they may not be asked to promote the product, achieve a lot of visibility, as does the company picking up their expenses. That makes them more electable for boards and national offices of the organization.

3. Publishers usually invite a panel of influential school people to serve as consultants on their programs. These educators and administrators often have minimal involvement in the production of the program, but their names, pictures, and affiliations appear in the books, lending them credibility. At the same time these consultants have a conflict of interest when basals are selected.

5

THE MAKING OF THE BASAL READER

It's clear from the discussion above that basal readers are regarded widely by professionals in education as a reliable technology for instruction devised by the best, most knowledgeable scientific authorities. In this next section we'll examine several questions. How are basals produced? Who produces the basals? Who are the people that make the basals into what they are and what are the forces that influence them?

HOW ARE BASALS PRODUCED?

The following scenario for production of a basal series draws on a study by Graham, using the techniques of investigative reporting, of two major publishers which he identified by fictitious names, Gorman House and Herculean Press (Graham,1978). Graham conducted in-depth, taped interviews with reading series personnel of the two publishing houses to obtain his information. What he found may be somewhat different at other publishers. And more use of computers

This plan for production of a new basal series starts and ends with marketing considerations.

and automation may take place now. Some components of current basals may actually be produced under subcontracts by independent companies which may be working for several publishers at the same time (McInnis, 1987). But this description corresponds with the personal experiences of a former basal author on which we have also drawn.

Graham discusses how a product plan is developed by the management of a basal publisher prior to getting approval for spending the millions necessary to produce a marketable series. This plan for production of a new basal series starts and ends with marketing considerations. The company calculates what the current market is, how many companies share this market and what potential share a new program can expect. Of greatest concern are factors that will affect market share, such as satisfaction of users with current programs, age of current programs, etc.

The company estimates the cost of producing the program, the potential selling price, and the profits if the program achieves varying segments of the total market. The life of a series is figured at about seven years. Costs can be manipulated by decisions on method of printing, kind and amount of color, use of freelance artists rather than staff artists. Only if the company can be reasonably sure of profits will they proceed to develop the program.

The publisher develops a product strategy. Which segment of the market is the program intended for? Usually publishers are interested in the largest segment. "For the most part, ... a major reading series market is comprised of all elementary and junior high students in the United States and all American students living abroad"(Graham p. 86).

The physical characteristics of the program must be determined with marketing personnel again taking the lead but with the cooperation of editorial production, and art representatives. Plans are made for the program's components, the annotated teachers' editions, the student anthologies, the workbooks, and the teachers' manuals. Decisions involve amount and type of art, number of levels and pages assigned to each level, the kind of paper, stitching, printing, binding. Cost of obtaining rights to stories and editing them is considered. The physical design is important because that essentially determines cost.

New programs emulate successful older programs.

Consideration of criteria for content again involves market analysis. The publisher wants to know which features of successful programs account for their success or failure. Market research companies are contracted to find out which features users value most. This is an essentially circular process: New programs emulate successful older programs. If some feature is cited by the market researchers as popular with buyers then the new program will attempt to outdo the competition on that dimension. When pre-primers, books with very few words which precede the primers, appeared in the early years of the basals, they became quite popular with buyers concerned about "readiness." So publishers could make their series attractive by offering more pre-primers with fewer words in each.

Publishers are also concerned with what reading educators are talking about in journals and at professional conferences. But they also watch carefully to see which terms and concepts pop up in their competitors' teachers' manuals. It's easier to talk about new concepts in teachers' manuals than it is to implement them in the programs, and there is little risk as long as no real change is involved. Graham reports one publisher as saying:

> You can't be too advanced, or educators won't buy it. You can't be too late with innovations or your competition will have beaten you to it. You have to be exactly on target.

In the plan, the publisher sets a target date for publication. Key factors involved are:

1. Deadlines for submission for adoption in key states and major school districts.
2. IRA convention dates.

Newness is a very important competitive factor, so, like automobiles, basal series often carry a copyright date a year in advance of actual marketing. If the series is ready in 1987 it will carry a 1988 copyright as the "official publication date." Similarly, revisions will be planned to give the program a new copyright date, and often a new title when it is being submitted for adoption in a major state or district.

The issue of deadlines is not a simple one. Setting unrealistic dates in order to meet adoption deadlines in a key state may increase costs. But missing a deadline may cause a loss of marketing momentum or give another publisher an advantage. In any case, publishers frequently find themselves rushed as their deadlines approach. There is abundant evidence in published materials that last minute pressures, among other factors, influence the quality of the programs in unplanned ways.

A calendar is set for all aspects of the development of the series and prices and sales targets are set for the components. "This calendar may consist of between thirty and sixty events over a three to five year period, depending on the magnitude of the program and on the groundwork that may have been previously laid if the series is a revision"(Graham, p. 93-94). This schedule is adjusted within limits. But, in general, as in all industry, heads roll when costly delays occur. Job security in publishing houses is not very high.

The company's product plan includes a section delineating the risks. What if the sales are not as good as projected? "We are a very conservative industry," Graham quotes the vice-president of Gorman House as saying (p. 94). In general, program decisions are made to reduce risk. And the risks are real, with millions invested before any income is received. Furthermore, there is a strong tendency to avoid making risky key decisions. Editors and executives will attempt to shift responsibility for these decisions up or down the line knowing that someone will take the blame if a decision is seen later as a costly mistake. Even the president or chairman of the board is not totally safe if an expensive program fails. So new programs tend to stay well within what their designers consider to be safe limits, avoiding risky innovations.

Author selection is one of the least important parts of putting together a series." Graham

The Role of the Authors

According to Graham the authors may not even be involved in any of the plan's development:

> On arriving at Gorman House for this study, the first question asked...was "How do you select your senior authors for the series?" The liaison laughed and said, "That is a very premature question, if you are really interested in what makes this business tick. Author selection is one of the least important parts of putting together a series."

Again, the marketing department plays a crucial role in choosing the authorship team. As Graham puts it, "A company product is being shaped, not an individual's ideas being transformed into a book"(p. 95). Perhaps there was a time (before 1960?) when key authors had a major hand in developing a series. Their current role is a good deal less clearly defined.

This is not to say that the authors are not knowledgeable, recognized authorities in the field of reading or in related fields, such as early childhood development, literature, linguistics, psychology, or cognitive science. Publishers seek authors who are widely recognized by teachers and others who may participate in adoption procedures. So they want people who have published articles, written college textbooks, spoken frequently at conferences and conducted in-services. An established research reputation is also a plus. But the publisher wants authors at least as much for their credibility and their ability and willingness to help promote sales once the series is published as for their actual contributions to the programs.

How much actual writing the authors will do is variable from series to series and even within authorship teams. Publishers generally find that they can control the time, content, and quality of writing better when it is done by people employed by them as editors. "...series houses have often cared more about the national prominence of their authors than about their actual ability" (Graham, p. 96). The in-house editors spend all their time working on the series. Authors are full-time educators who have far less time to devote to the basal. Furthermore, to gain prominence, potential authors usually have had to obtain senior professorial rank at universities where they are expected to spend their time writing articles and doing research. Authoring elementary-school textbooks does not count for much in the academic marketplace. So such authors are generally pleased with playing the role of senior advisors, planning with the editorial staff, critiquing the materials, and writing scholarly inserts for teachers' manuals.

Another factor in choosing authors is their availability. The publisher wants to be assured that they will be available during the time the series is being written and that they are not overcommitted, a real problem for highly prominent authorities in the field. Publishers try to make contact with younger researchers and authorities, hoping that their prominence will increase by the time the series is published and established.

Publishers are also influenced by race, ethnicity, geographic region, and other demographic factors in choosing their authorship teams. One way to achieve diversity is to designate a wider group as consultants and advisors. These are often people in administrative positions in local or state school authorities. That also gives another kind of credibility. They should know the realities of the classroom.

Though a successful series may sell millions of dollars worth a year, that doesn't mean that today's basal authors are growing immensely wealthy on their royalties. Whereas college text authors are paid 10 to 15 percent of the net price as royalty, the authors of basals share about 4 percent. With proceeds for the top programs in multi-million dollar figures, even that is no small amount. But there may be several authors listed on each text in addition to senior authors. Each will share in this royalty pool so that the actual royalty paid to any given author may not be a very large percent of the sales. Those whose names appear as advisors or consultants may get only a one-time fee or a small annual retainer.

Who Are the Editors?

Most editors are not highly paid. They may be former teachers and their salaries are comparable to what teachers make, not higher. They work a fifty week year. Editors don't have much power either. The editors work within policies set by the management ostensibly with the consent of the authors. "Editors do not have much influence over the structure of the reading program, but it is their language that guides teachers through the lessons" (Graham, p. 125).

Usually there are several levels of editors starting as trainee and moving through assistants, associates, editors, supervising editors, executive editors, and editors-in-chief. At each higher level somewhat more authority and decision-making may be permitted by the company. Most of the actual writing of the teachers' manuals, the lessons, the questions, and the workbook exercises is done by junior-level editors working within tight specifications. Top-level editors may have participated in laying out the key aspects of these specifications and will have fleshed them out for those who will be responsible for executing the plan. But key marketing people have more influence over these specifications than most of the authors or editors.

Editors, like teachers, work from their own intuitions

"Editors do not have much influence over the structure of the reading program, but it is their language that guides teachers through the lessons." (Graham)

about what is best for pupils at a particular point. Unlike teachers, however, they do not have any feedback from a group of learners. They can, if they wish, arrange with nearby schools to try out materials with students. That's time-consuming and rarely done in any systematic way during program development.

Usually different components of the basals, particularly the tests, are written by separate groups of editors. Teams of editors are assigned to work simultaneously on the different basal components and levels. Supervising editors attempt to keep all this coordinated to produce a cohesive program. But that's not always easy, particularly as deadlines approach.

In theory the tests are based on the same criteria as the program, particularly the skill components, but that doesn't mean they are always closely keyed to the rest of the program. The test-item writers are preoccupied with test theory and formulas for generating items. Since these are objective or criterion- rather than norm-referenced tests they do not necessarily require trials with pupils. Sometimes there is an analysis done of the test results, but that can only really be done after the program is in use. It may result in some revision of some items on subsequent printings.

Finalizing the Plan

By the time the product plan is ready to present to top management for final approval and funding it will contain details of (Graham, p. 100):

  an exhaustive analysis of competing series
  the organization of the proposed series
  the teacher aid features
  the lesson developments
  skill developments
  media components
  design for components and linking features of the
      physical designs
  description of content and price
  a rationale for each instructional feature, each skill

and precisely where it will be taught
complete specifications of "learning outcomes" and
how they will be tested.

Selecting Content

Once the plan is funded, work begins in selecting
and developing content. Though publishers work hard
to include a range of selections written by well-known
children's authors, most of what eventually winds up
in the pupils' anthology to be read by the pupils is either adapted or specially written for the purpose. The
authors of previously published children's stories selected for inclusion and for which permission is needed
are certainly not getting rich. Graham reports an average of $500 paid for stories and $150 for poems, which
is then shared by the author and the original publisher.

Most of the material in the kindergarten and first-
grade levels is written by staff members. In the basals
of the 1930s through the 1950s, the members of a sub-
urban family were the continuing characters in these
staff-written stories. Dick and Jane and their counterparts, Tom and Betty, and the others, were supposed to
give young children characters with whom to identify.
Mother and Father provided strong sex identification
and role models. That was when Freudian psychology
was an important influence. In more recent years ethnic and socioeconomic diversity has appeared, and
Mother is out of her aprons and Father has taken off his
dress shirt and tie. But the texts themselves are still
synthesized from the word lists and readability formulas that grew out of the research of the 1920s.

Starting often in second grade and beyond most of
the material is from literature already published for
children, but it has been adapted. Publishers start out
seeking the best available material to make the program attractive to young readers and those who select
series for use. So editors follow the reviews of books
carefully. They pay attention to which authors are win-

*Most of what
eventually winds
up in the pupils'
anthology to be
read by the pupils
is either adapted
or specially
written for the
purpose.*

Each selection is read and edited at least forty times in the process, as it is "pounded into house requirements." Graham

ning awards and selling best. Under pressure from minorities and women's groups they look for a broad representation of people, cultures, lifestyles.

But then the process of selection and adaptation begins. There are two major types of adaptation. The first is adaptation to fit the readability and skill criteria of the publisher. Selections may be abridged, simplified, or rewritten. Vocabulary may be changed, sentences shortened, and story line modified. The key is to make the selections fit the charts developed for each grade. This is no small task and, even in the hands of skillful editors, it often results in relatively unnatural texts. The second kind of adaptation is to make the material fit standards of acceptability for content, language, and values. In general this is a kind of self-censorship to avoid offending a wide range of groups, from those concerned about racism and sexism to those who see witches, Communists, and secular humanists lurking in children's literature. Even selections which will only be listed for suggested further reading are purged if anyone thinks they might be offensive.

During the process of editing the series there is a continuous winnowing out and re-editing of the selections. Graham estimates that each selection is read and edited at least forty times in the process, as it is "pounded into house requirements" (p. 105). Screening editors pass selections on to supervising editors who may tentatively assign them to grade levels. Then factors such as genre, content, location, ethnic representation, sex of characters, readability rating, and ethnicity of the author is noted to seek a balance.

Editors higher up the chain of command as well as series authors may also consider the selections.

Ironically, with all this passing back and forth of the story, it is rare that children are brought into the process for their reactions or readings. In fact, the books will almost always be in print before a child has an opportunity to respond to them, and it is only if teachers report these responses that they may have any impact on subsequent revisions.

Graham estimates that only 10 percent of what is reviewed is actually used. Our own review of current basals indicates that, with the exception of an occasional poem, what is used is almost always adapted more or less severely. Sometimes this revision only involves an occasional word change or abridging. But often it would be hard for the original author to recognize the story.

Art and Physical Aspects

The artwork is carefully planned and co-ordinated by the publisher's art editors. Most of the artwork is done by artists paid by the illustration ($150-200 each, according to Graham, p. 144). As much as 25 percent of the page space may be illustration. Reproduction techniques have improved considerably, even including the brightness and quality of the covers which are now often pictorial. One place where publishers can compete is in the quality of the artwork, particularly the color processes. The visual impression the series makes on potential users is considered to be very important. No publisher can afford to be outdone by another in color quality or in the appeal of the illustrations.

Even physical characteristics of basals aren't safely noncontroversial. One publisher felt it suffered because it went to single-color covers to emphasize the "systems" nature of the series. Using a block nonindented paragraph also lost them sales, they felt. Some states require hardcover rather than softcover books, even in the first grade, which makes it impractical to produce separately bound "little books" as New Zealand has done very successfully.

The one area in which school consumers have been able to establish and enforce standards for school texts is in durability. The National Association of State Textbook Administrators (NASTA) provides guidelines for

Even physical characteristics of basals aren't safely noncontroversial.

printing and binding of texts. Publishers are required to submit samples for testing. Paper, endsheets, reinforcements, adhesives, stitching, cover board, and cover materials are all tested. Every component except the teachers' manual is covered(Graham, p. 138). It's interesting that purchasers have not sought to specify the content and methodology represented within these covers.

Basal publishers have from time-to-time considered how computers, compact discs, teaching machines and other nontext technology can augment or replace the current technology centered around hardcover books. But they have never been able to design or price out such programs. At best, what is produced are some supplementary materials that replace the workbooks and exercise materials of the basals with programmed and/or computerized versions of the same workbook-like exercises.

Squire provides the following breakdown for the portion of the sales dollar represented by cost factors:

26.5 percent for printing and product
12.2 percent for plant cost (investment in plate)
34.6 percent for marketing cost, "including the free teacher manuals and inspection copies, the staff development service as well as the freebies so deplored in this report"
8 percent goes for "fulfillment and inventory"
10 percent for administration
8.3 percent for editorial costs (including field testing and research)
4.2 percent in authors'royalties (Squire, 1987).

SUMMARY: THE MAKING OF THE BASALS

Basal readers are produced in the United States by an industry that operates like every other American industry. These are companies which appear on the major stock exchanges. They exist to make profits. What makes the basal reader unusual as a product of a profit-making industry is that it is regarded by the people who buy and use it as a product with intrinsic scientific integrity. There are other such products. NASA made its rockets appear to be so scientific that people came to regard them as infallible. Not until one exploded tragically before our eyes, instantly killing its crew, did the public reconsider that there was still much to be learned.

Basal readers don't explode. Teachers using them become comfortable with them even if they are never completely satisfied. The aura of science surrounding them, their slick attractive packaging, and the prestige of the authors make teachers lay the blame for any lack of success on themselves or their pupils and not on the basals.

The editors who do the bulk of the work in producing the basals are skilled professionals at what they do. What they do is operate within a framework which is closely based on existing successful programs. Except for the most senior editors they are not in a position to question key aspects of that framework. Authors, particularly senior authors, may be in a position to argue for shifts in philosophy or changes in methodology. But actual decisions are made by the management of the publishing house and, short of withdrawing from the authorship team, there is no way authors can decline to support these management decisions. Many authors have taken the path of resignation. But the contracts they have signed make it possible for their names to appear on materials they have worked on long after they have severed their relationships with the program.

At best the process of producing basals is a highly conservative one. It inhibits any real change or innovation as it seeks to minimize risks to sales and profits. That makes it hard for authors, editors, or even management to incorporate newly discovered knowledge from theory and research, since the potential response of selection committees cannot be predicted safely.

A vicious circle makes the process even more conservative. School administrators are also likely to avoid

At best the process of producing basals is a highly conservative one.

risks involved in committing to innovation. So sales staff and market researchers report to corporate planners that potential purchasers prefer familiar, safe materials. This circle can only be broken when schools begin to turn away from basals or at least severely modify their use. Ironically, only when publishers' market research tells them that there is at least as much economic risk in staying with existing formulas as moving to new ones can there be any major change in the basals

6

THE NATURE OF THE CONTEMPORARY BASAL

To provide a complete picture of the contemporary American basal reader, several popular current series were critically examined using the Program Profile Instrument developed by Goodman and Page (1978) as the central tool. We draw on that analysis and a parallel one of Spanish-language basals in the United States (Freeman, 1986) to provide a profile of the contemporary basal. Though this profile will be illustrated with examples from specific basals, we will not provide an in-depth description of any single program.

USING WORDS AND SKILLS AS SEQUENCABLE COMPONENTS

The reliance on Thorndyke's Laws of Learning requires a view of reading which makes it possible to break it down into sequencable components that can be controlled and explicitly taught. This is a requirement of the program itself. Reading is defined in such a way that there will be the necessary control criteria for the

A major organiz-
ing principle of
basal readers is
that learning to
read is, more than
anything else,
learning words
and skills for
identifying words.

basal program. This is not to say that there could not be other programs that are organized on some other premises and which do not require a sequencable definition of reading. Such programs can and do exist. Consider, for example, Bill Martin, Jr.'s, *Sounds of Language* which is essentially a series of literature anthologies. But such programs have typically been labeled as supplemental and not basal by their publishers in the United States. By definition, at the present time, a basal must have sequencable components.

READING AS IDENTIFYING WORDS

Since Thorndyke's research on word frequency, the American basal reader has been essentially word-centered. A major organizing principle of basal readers is that learning to read is, more than anything else, learning words and skills for identifying words. Though there is considerable focus on phonics in all the basals, even when a series is labeled as a phonics program the emphasis is on words, with phonics as a means of "decoding" or identifying the words. Lippincott Basic Reading, for example, claims that as a result of the teaching of five vowels and eleven consonants in Book A, 240 words are taught.

Though all programs use contexts of varying length and to varying degrees, the focus is on using context to identify words.

Controlled Vocabulary

All basals use controlled vocabulary as a major sequencing element. Vocabulary in the readers is chosen from lists such as those compiled by Thorndyke of the most frequent words. The introduction of these words is carefully controlled so that each new word is repeated several times and only a few are introduced at a time. A cumulative word list is provided at the back of each book in the series. In the pre-primers, the first "books" of the program, stories are created from the words introduced in this way. Here is an example:

The editors and/or authors are primarily concerned with controlling the introduction of words.

We Can Go

I can go.	I will go.
Can you go?	I will help you.
Help! Help!	You can not help.
I can not go.	
I will help you.	Can you go?
You can go.	I can.
	We can go.
	We can.

(Houghton, Level B, Pre-Primer)

In these beginning levels the editors and/or authors are primarily concerned with controlling the introduction of words. They then produce synthetic "stories" such as this composed of words explicitly "taught." The accompanying illustrations carry the story line and provide what content and cohesion is possible. This text relates to a series of pictures of a child's attempts at roller-skating. The story told by the pictures makes some sense to pupils. The words in this text are, with the exception of *help* and *go*, function words and first and second person pronouns which have exophoric reference (in the pictures). The text is not natural language (it could not occur outside of this pre-primer genre) and it is therefore unpredictable for the learner. The intent is to teach these words which, because they are common, will then be useful in reading more natural, interesting, and meaningful texts.

Here's another example from another series. This story is accompanied by cartoonlike illustrations. In each picture the central character, a pan, is depicted as a cast-iron skillet with a human face. Additionally, each time one of the characters in the text speaks, a small head of the character appears before the lines. And each time certain key words appear the word is superimposed on a small picture of what the word represents. In the example such illustrated words are in brackets.

The Happy Pan

(Boy)	I will make a cake in the pan.
(Pan)	But cake is not good for a happy pan.
	I want a [plant]
	The pan ran to get a [plant]
	A mouse saw the pan.
	The mouse put the pan into the lake.
(Mouse)	I like boats.
	The pan is a good boat.
(Pan)	But I want to get a [plant]
	The pan ran to get a [plant]

In the story this pattern is repeated as the pan is captured by a bear who uses it as a kite, and the skillet is portrayed frowning but flying. Again the kite/pan escapes, floats weightlessly through a window where a girl is potting a plant. The pan smiles as the girl pots the plant in the pan. On the last page the pan summarizes:

(Pan)	The boy has no cake pan.
	The mouse has no boat.
	The bear has no kite.
	But I have a [plant]
	A [plant] is good for a happy pan!

Scott, Foresman, *Focus*, 1985

In this same series a version of the classic folktale, *Little Red Ridinghood* appears. Here are the first few pages of that rendition.

Red Ridinghood wants to see Grandma.
(RR)I can put apples into my [basket].

I can put red apples into
   my [basket] for Grandma.

I will walk to see Grandma.
I like to hear the red [bird].
Grandma likes to hear the [bird].
Grandma will come out to hear
   the red [bird].

(Wolf) Hello, Red Ridinghood, Hello.

(RR) I have red apples.
I have big red apples for Grandma.
I put the apples into my [basket].

(Wolf) Red Ridinghood will walk
   to see Grandma.
I will not walk.
I will run to see Grandma.

Notice in this story that there is more concern for controlling the vocabulary than telling the story. Words like red, bird, apples are repeated even when they are inappropriate to the story line. This is emphasized by the last page. After the woodcutter has chased the wolf away and saved her life, Red Ridinghood proclaims:

There is more concern for controlling the vocabulary than telling the story.

(RR) I like you, Woodcutter.
Come have some apples.
I put red apples into my [basket].
I put big red apples into
[basket]. (sic)

When the program is trying to control both vocabulary and phonics the synthetic text shows both influences. Words are introduced to provide practice for the letter-sound relationships which have been introduced.

Here's a selection from the Economy Reading Series.

The Dog in the Van

<u>Did</u> I see a dog?
I did!
The dog <u>went</u> into the <u>van.</u>
Did I see a <u>red</u> dog?
Is the dog red?

Is a dog in the van?
Is it red?
Is a red dog in the van?

I did not paint the dog.
I did not paint Happy.
Happy went into the paint.

The dog is red.
The paint made it red.
I did see a red dog.
It went into the van.
A red dog is in the van.

Economy, Level C, Pre-Primer

The underlined words are words used for the first time in the program. Though this is a program with a strong phonics emphasis, teachers are instructed to use word cards to drill children on these words before reading the story (Economy, p. 109).

*Behavioral Laws
of Learning led to
the view that
reading is learned
a word, a sound,
or a skill at a
time.*

SKILLS AND HABITS IN THE SCOPE AND SEQUENCE

Language has been the object of study by scholars from the time of the ancient Greeks to the present. In recent decades it has been the concern of scholars and researchers from a wide variety of disciplines and lively controversies continue in several of these. One major dispute is whether language is habitual, whether it is innate, or whether it is a personal-social invention. The first view, espoused by behavioral psychologists, is that language is habitual behavior learned through responses to environmental stimuli. The second view, most recently espoused by linguists such as Noam Chomsky and cognitive psychologists such as Eric Lenneberg, is that human beings are born with an innate language competence which is then particularized in contact with the language of the family and community. The third view, notably advanced by Michael Halliday (1985), a linguist, and Lev Vygotsky (1978), a Russian psychologist, is that language is a social invention internalized by children as they transact with family and other members of the language community.

Today's basal readers still largely represent the view of language as habit that was broadly accepted by the psychologists of the 1920s who helped shape the basals. Behavioral Laws of Learning led to the view that reading is learned a word, a sound, or a skill at a time. That's why there is so strong an emphasis in basals on a sequence of words and the skills for attacking them.

Separable Strands

This view of language as habit can be seen in the scope and sequence charts of the basals and in the heavy emphasis in the programs on drill and practice. Each program defines its scope in a series of separable strands, within which are skill and sub-skill sequences which are explicitly assigned to levels (and or school grades). Exercises are aimed at development of each skill and assessment is heavily focussed on skill mastery.

Ginn(1985) has four major strands in their program:

1. Decoding
2. Vocabulary
3. Comprehension
4. Life and study skill

Scott, Foresman(1985) states these "principles":

1. Develop pupil ability to identify words.
2. Develop pupil ability to comprehend meanings (literal and implied) of words, phrases, whole sentences.
3. Develop pupil ability to study effectively.
4. Develop an interest in and love of reading.
5. Help pupils use what they have learned in other language and creative experiences.

Houghton Mifflin (1986) has these scope and sequence categories:

1. Decoding/phonics
2. Comprehension
3. Reference and study
4. Literary skills
5. Vocabulary
6. Language.

Economy (1986), though considered a phonics emphasis program, has a similar set of strands:

1. Vocabulary
2. Comprehension
3. Decoding
4. Literary
5. Study skills/life skills

There is consistency in two respects in the strands each basal provides. The lists are remarkably similar in their terminology and they are similar in their focus on part to whole, bottom up sequence. Though there is some concern in all the basals for meaning and context,

This view of language as habit can be seen in the scope and sequence charts of the basals

Only 10 to 15 percent of the instructional time will actually be spent in silent reading of cohesive texts.

there is more concern with controlling the sequence of sounds, words, and skills than in providing authentic language in texts. Much of the artificiality and lack of cohesion in the basal examples cited above comes from this preoccupation with parts and sequence.

Lesson Sequences

The organization of lessons is keyed to practicing skills. The story is there as a means of focussing on and practicing the skills and learning the words, which are the real object of instruction.

Heath's three-part lesson plan is typical:

A. Preparation for reading: teaching and practice activities develop skill to be applied in reading.
B. Reading and comprehending: story discussion, teaching, practice activities integrate comprehension skills with selection readings. This combines skill learning with reading.
C. Reteaching and enrichment.

Houghton Mifflin uses a three-part lesson, but varies the sequence because the third part of each lesson is preparation for the reading in the next lesson. Holt's three parts are preparing to read, reading and comprehending, and developing and applying skills. One reason why there is this three-part division in the lesson sequence is the common use of three ability groups in reading classrooms. Each group can be at a different phase of the lesson sequence so the teacher can be with the group that is doing the guided reading portion while other students use work in the workbook or skill sheets.

This may sound as if about one-third of the instructional time devoted to reading is actually spent in reading. However, the third of the lesson devoted to reading and comprehension is actually also likely to be divided into three parts: introducing the selection, guiding the reading, and following up the reading. During the reading there are also questions to be answered. In the programs we studied, it is likely that only 10 to 15 percent of the instructional time will actually be spent in silent reading of cohesive texts.

Durkin remarks of her study of basals:

> That the readers in a basal series constitute the core of the program was not supported either. In fact, the little instruction offered in the manuals, as well as the large amount of practice recommended, only rarely were related to selections in the readers. Lessons often consisted, therefore, of a sequence of suggestions about topics with no relationship to what the children were reading and no relationship to each other (Durkin, 1987, p. 337).

COMPONENTS

Every series, as we have indicated, is made of many components. Chiefly these are the sequenced anthologies, or readers, workbooks and practice materials, and a variety of tests. All programs also offer many optional components. The whole is co-ordinated through the teachers' manuals.

FITTING LITERATURE INTO THE SEQUENCE

In later basal levels, where real texts from children's literature are used, controlled vocabulary is a major criterion for revising texts.

Words already introduced in the series and those high on the published frequency lists are substituted for less common words in the texts.

In the following example of a revised sequence from a Judy Blume selection many of the factors we discussed when we talked about how basal editors adapt selections for the basal are evident. The character *Freddie* has become a girl, *Maggie,* probably to get a better gender balance. *Ellen* has been promoted to older sister, and *Mike* is now the little brother. These are not the only character name changes. *Ms. Gumber,* Freddie/Maggie's teacher in the original, becomes *Mrs. Cook* in the revision. This carries through an old tradi-

In the process of controlling the vocabulary and syntax, the style and wit of the original is lost.

tion in basals to use real words as proper last names wherever possible. That stems from the view that exposure to a word is extra practice no matter where it occurs in the text. The drama teacher moves from *Ms. Matson* to *Mrs. Chang* in the revision. Here the goal apparently is ethnic balance. The thread of sibling rivalry and the hostile feelings and actions of the three siblings toward each other are carefully censored in this beginning passage and throughout the remainder of the story.

The biggest change is the reduction of the text through the avoidance of less frequent words and the use of short sentences. In the process of controlling the vocabulary and syntax, the style and wit of the original is lost, and the language becomes much less natural and thus less predictable.

> Freddie Dissel had two problems. One was his older brother Mike. The other was his younger sister Ellen. Freddy thought a lot about being the one in the middle. But there was nothing he could do about it. He felt like the peanut butter part of a sandwich, squeezed between Mike and Ellen.
>
> Original: (Blume,1981)

> Maggie had a big sister, Ellen.
> She had a little brother, Mike.
> Maggie was the one in the middle.
> And she didn't like it.
> But what could she do?
>
> Revision: (Holt, Level 8, Grade 1)

Focus on Learning Words

Word lists are provided in the basals for every story so that the teachers and learners will know which words are to be learned. This use of stories from literature to teach words is also illustrated in the preparation the basal directs teachers to use *before the story is read.* For example, under the heading, "Developing Vocabulary," pupils are focussed on particular words before they read "Maggie in the Middle." The stated objectives are:

To increase a basic reading vocabulary.
To understand the direct, literal meaning of a sentence.
To apply decoding skills previously learned.

Two types of words are singled out: "Special Attention Words"—*Maggie, middle, Ellen, clothes, room, away;* "Easily Decoded Words" *Mike, Ellen, fit, ones, own, run, Maggie's."* It is not clear what criteria are used to differentiate between the two classifications. The teacher is instructed to place the new words on the chalkboard or in pocket charts. Then an instructional sequence is provided for each word.

For example:

Display the word *middle.*
Have the children notice the double consonants and the *le* ending that is pronounced as it is in <u>little</u>. Then have them read the words in this sentence.
Maggie is in the <u>middle</u>.

(p. T-133)

In the margin of each reproduced page from the pupil's text in the teachers' manual, again under the heading of "Vocabulary Development," is a note for each of these introduced words as they occur. For example:

Mike

Decode *Mike* by combining the initial /m/ as in the picture-word *man* with the graphemic base *-ike.*

(p. T-134 rel. to p. 88).

On the last page of the selection to be read the teachers' manual offers a review exercise for "Vocabulary Reinforcement." Each of the "special attention words" is again to be written on the board. Then the teacher reads sentences with missing words and asks the children to fill in the blanks by pointing to and reading the missing words. The sentences are not sentences from the story.

Next the teacher writes all the "easily decodable words" on the board and reads a series of words that rhymes with those, asking children to point to and read the word that rhymes with each (*i.e., fiddle/middle*).

The focus of the instruction is on words, before, during, and after the story.

The focus of the instruction is on words, before, during, and after the story. But the word focus does not stop there. A workbook sequence follows where exercises are designed to teach the pupils, explicitly, the skills for "decoding" words: the vowel sound /y/ in a group of words, consonants /b/ /d/ /g/ /l/ /m/ in beginning, middle, and final position in a group of words. Other exercises ask students to substitute pronouns for nouns and work with contractions. These exercises are not related to the text the children are reading.

COMPREHENSION AS SKILLS

All of the series indicate that comprehension is part of reading. One program Harper and Row, Lippincott Basic Reading (sub-titled a *Phonic/Linguistic Series*) (1981), identifies three meanings for reading (Lippincott, 1981). The first is building on known phonetic elements to decode familiar words. The second definition comes as students master the decoding process and expand their reading vocabulary. Readers then use literal, inferential, and evaluative skills to develop understanding. After decoding ability and skills of understanding are acquired, students can recognize and appreciate the special value of literature.

Reading Comprehension Follows and Is Separable from Identifying Words

The view, that understanding is separable from and dependent on the development of word identification abilities and a vocabulary of known words, is not explicitly asserted in all basals. It is implicit in how they organize their lessons and how they list their objectives and priorities.

Each of the basals treat comprehension as composed of a series of skills. They also categorize comprehension as having several sub-components. Sometimes the terms for the skills and the components seem to over-lap. Questions before and during the reading are usual-ly labeled to fit these skill and/or component categories. For "Maggie in the Middle," (Holt, cited above), under a heading of "Comprehension/Literary Skills," these objectives for the story are listed: Reading vocabulary, Sentence meaning, Cause and effect, Re-calling details: characters. Here vocabulary is included under comprehension and separately from phoni-cs/decoding.

These questions appear in the teachers' manual for the first page of the story under the heading, "Compre-hension Checkup":

Each of the basals treat comprehension as composed of a series of skills.

Literal Understanding	1. How did Maggie feel about being in the middle? (She didn't like it.) **Characterization.**
Inferential Thinking	2. Who is bigger, Ellen or Maggie? (Ellen) **Drawing Conclusions**
Critical Thinking	3. Can you think of some good things about being a middle child? (You have someone older to help you and some-one younger who may need your help. Answers will vary.) **Background Knowledge**

For each page of this story there are almost as many questions in the comprehension check-up as sentences in the story. There is a question paradigm being fol-lowed here, which we found typical of the basals we examined, that appears to be grounded in a view that children comprehend to the extent that they agree with the question writer's view of the text meaning. Even when the question is intended to draw on "back-ground knowledge" and require "critical thinking" a simple conformist answer is suggested as a model for the teacher of acceptable answers. It is frequently hard to see consistency in the categorization of the ques-tions, particularly when, as in this series, each question is put in a single category.

The issue of conformity to a predetermined answer

is not a minor one, and it is complicated by a tendency for questions and answers to be inappropriate to the text. The question: "Who is bigger, Ellen or Maggie?" seems simple and straightforward. But children know that a *big* sister is not the same as a *bigger* sister. Furthermore, the pictures on the page with the text show a much larger view of Maggie with a smaller picture of Ellen as if behind her. On the second page of the story there's a more serious problem. The picture shows Maggie bundled up in coat, scarf, cap, and mittens. The text says:

Ellen got too big for her clothes.
Ellen's clothes fit Maggie.
Maggie got the old clothes.
Ellen got new ones.

Two questions, both labeled "inferential thinking," relate to this sequence.

---

1. Why does Maggie look funny in the picture?
(Because the clothes she is wearing are too big.)
Picture Clues
2. Why is Maggie wearing clothes that are too big?
(Because she is wearing her sister Ellen's clothes, which Ellen has outgrown.)
Cause and Effect

The text says Ellen's clothes fit Maggie, and though the picture may suggest otherwise, the "literal" response the pupils might make is likely to be at odds with the inference the question writer expects them to make. The intention here is not to find petty flaws in the basals. But what emerges in the examination of the questions used in assessing comprehension in these basals is a sense that the categorization system has not been used well and the questions themselves are often questionable. Since both the teaching and assessment of comprehension in the basals are confined almost entirely to the questions the teachers are instructed to use, the quality of the questions must be a major concern.

The basals present an image of order, system, and science which disappears as it is pursued in its application.

This suggests a problem noted by others: The basals present an image of order, system, and science which disappears as it is pursued in its application. Durkin reports that after her undergraduate class had made an in-depth examination of one lesson sequence from a second grade basal, her students responses could be summarized in this comment: "It really takes time and work to turn these lessons into something worth doing. No wonder so many teachers just use them as they are"(Durkin, 1987, p. 340).

Ginn provides a key to a code system it uses to label questions in the teachers' manual for their series:

E Experiential   I Inferential   L Literal
AP Author's Purpose   CE Cause/Effect   CH Character   CM Comparison
D Details   DC Drawing Conclusions   FO Fact/Opinion   FL Figurative Language
MI Main Idea   PO Predicting Outcomes   RF Reality/Fantasy
R Referents   S Sequence   SD Supporting Details

In the teachers' manual for one third-grade story, "Alvin's Masterpiece," under the heading "Reading for Comprehension," there are one to three questions for the teacher to ask for each page in the pupil's text. Here are the questions for the first two pages :

How would you describe the way Alvin painted.
(I—DC, MI   *He was a very sloppy painter.*)
What did Alvin think of his painting at first?
(I—SD,DC   *He thought it was his best.*)
What happened to Alvin's painting as he continued to work?
(L—SD   *It got worse and worse.*)

This text asks fewer questions per line of pupil text than the one discussed before it. The questions can apparently serve more than one purpose as the first does: an inferential question that deals with drawing conclusions and main idea. But it is hard to find reasons for

Most of the "teaching" of comprehension is through the use of questions before, during, and after the reading.

the first two being labeled inference and the third literal. The single correct answers are not precisely out of the wording of the text. The text says that paint would fly onto his paper, his shirt, his pants so the reader is to describe the way he painted as sloppy, an inference. "My oh my! This is fantastic," Alvin is quoted as saying in the text. That should, according to the manual, lead the reader to infer: "He thought it was his best." "But the painting wasn't getting any better. It had been much better before..." is what the text says. That is to be literally understood as meaning: "It got worse and worse." Why do the first two questions involve drawing conclusions while the last is only supporting detail?

It appears that the writers and classifiers of these questions had difficulty using the system in a consistent manner. Furthermore, the answer to the second question seems unwarranted. That's a problem if comprehension is to be judged by the students' abilities to produce answers that match the correct response in the manual.

Comprehension as Product, not Process

Recent reading comprehension theory is discussed in many of the teachers' materials in basal programs, and a clear impression is given that comprehension is stressed in the programs. But most of the "teaching" of comprehension is through the use of questions before, during, and after the reading of the stories. Durkin, in her study of the teaching of comprehension, finds it essential "to call attention to the difference between teaching comprehension, which is concerned with the process of comprehending, and assessing or testing comprehension, whose concern lies with the product(s) of comprehending." She differentiates further teaching and facilitating comprehension, though she sees both as concerned with process (Durkin, 1987, p. 336).

Durkin found that less than 1 percent of the time of

thirty-nine third- to sixth-grade teachers was spent on comprehension instruction, while 18 percent was spent on assessment and 15 percent on giving comprehension assignments. That led Durkin to examine the manuals of five basal readers for evidence of concern for reading comprehension as process. She found little she could label instruction. Instead she found an emphasis on practice unrelated to the selections in the readers and "numerous assessment questions that teachers were supposed to ask both during and after reading the selection. One or two other questions usually stated indirectly, were commonly referred to as purpose-setting questions. It was not uncommon, as a matter of fact, to find as many as 30 questions and a dozen references to practice exercises for as little as an eight-page basal selection" (Durkin, 1987, p. 337).

We found, as did Durkin, that the questions in basals tended to require single correct answers directly from the text. In the Holt series, for example, when we checked the questions for one story in each of several levels, we found that the proportion of questions asked during and after reading each selection with single correct answers was high, varying from 63 to 98 percent. There is no easily discernible pattern in the variations (see Table 1).

Less than 1 percent of the time of thirty-nine third- to sixth-grade teachers was spent on comprehension instruction.

Table 1   Text Questions with Single Correct Answers

Level	Grade	Questions in percents		Single Answers in percents	Variable Answers in percents	
4 (pre-primer)	1st	18	16	88.89	2	11.11
6 (pre-primer)	1st	31	23	74.19	8	25.81
7 (primer)	1st	54	34	62.96	20	37.04
8	1st	41	29	70.73	12	29.27
11	3rd	20	17	85.00	3	15.00
12	3rd	31	25	80.65	6	19.35
14	5th	42	41	97.62	1	2.38

Contemporary multidisciplinary research is producing a view of reading comprehension as an active, transactional, and constructive process, one in which

Basals, in their treatment of language, have tended to isolate sounds, letters, and words from these systems.

readers construct meaning as they transact with the text. This involves the reader in drawing on schemas built through past experience to make sense of the text. It is clear that the producers of the basals are not unaware of this emerging consensus. Articles and short commentaries included in the teachers' manuals of some of the basals reflect aspects of this transactional view. Some of these are written by authors of the particular programs. But the basals do not reflect the influence of this view except in choice of terminology. The focus of the basals is not on supporting development of the strategies for comprehending; rather it remains on the products of comprehension represented by the students' abilities to produce "correct" answers to arbitrary questions.

Fracturing and Narrowing Language

Another concern in the theoretical literature of the past decades has been on what makes language language and what makes a text a text. Linguists generally agree that to be language there must be three systems present. In Halliday's terms these three levels are the symbolic system (phonology in speech, orthography in writing), the lexico-grammatical system, and the meaning system. The middle system includes both the wording of the text and its structure (Halliday, 1985).

Basals, in their treatment of language, have tended to isolate sounds, letters, and words from these systems. They have given little attention to the systems and how they relate in natural texts. In pulling out letter-sound relationships these become distorted abstractions. Words out of context lose textual meaning and grammatical function. They also become abstractions. Furthermore, the value of the information in the parts is not the same as it is in the whole natural text. The whole is more than the sum of its parts and system gives unity to the whole.

If we compare the beginnings of the original and revised versions of the Judy Blume story above we get a sense of what makes a text a text and why focus on parts rather than the whole makes language less predictable and less comprehensible to readers. There are reasons why stories are worded the way they are. Some of them have to do with the style and voice of the author. But some of them have to do with the way the system of language works.

In basal programs language is not likely to be authentic language; that is, it is not likely to be a functional cohesive text which has a communicative purpose for the reader and which is embedded in a real literacy event. Pupils are continually encountering reduced language shaped to fit the scope and sequence chart. Even when what they are assigned to read starts out as a real story written by a real author, it is likely that it has been transformed considerably before the child encounters it.

There is a narrowing of focus from pupil anthologies to the workbooks and skill practice materials and then to the tests. Simply speaking, while the teachers'manuals can suggest somewhat more interactive and holistic concerns with the reading of the anthology selections, the workbooks focus on skills; use shorter, less complete contexts; and reduce reading instruction focus to parts rather than the whole. The tests carry this reduction further as they narrow their focus to what can be easily measured with paper and pencil. It also makes a difference that different people are responsible for each component in the creating of the basals. The narrowing effect is heightened by this specialization.

Increasing Word Focus

There is an increasing focus on words and word identification as the program moves from the anthology to the workbook and other instructional exercise and practice components. Here's the first part of a selection.

The Friends Help

Kim went to fix the wagon.
Jack went to help.
And Kim's friends went to help

Ted said, "I can fix the wagon."
Ted sat down in the grass.
Fay said, "I can help!
I can."

Jack said, "Fay is little.
Can Fay help?"
Kim said, "Fay is not little.
Fay can help fix the wagon."

(Harcourt, Level 2, p. 2)

In the workbook designed to be used with this story is the page in Figure 1. The directions to the teacher indicate it provides practice in "visual discrimination of sentences."

Figure 1 Workbook Exercise

What is in the box?
The hat was in the box.
The hat is in the box.
The hat is in a pond.
The hat is in the box.
(hat picture)

The bee was not a help.
The bee was not a help.
The bee was not a help.
The bee is not a help.
The bee was not a help.
(bee picture)

The duck was in the box.
The dog was in the pond.
The duck was in the box.
The duck sat in the box.
The duck was in the box.
(duck picture)

The turtle got up to help.
The turtle got up and ran.
The turtle got up and hid.
The turtle got up to help.
The turtle got a big box.
(turtle picture)

(Harcourt Program)

The directions for pupils in the workbook tell them to underline every sentence that is the same as the underlined sentence at the top. Notice that there is much less context here than in the synthetic story. Note also that *help* appears only as a verb in the story, but here it appears as a noun in a position where *helper* would be much more predictable.

Because of the emphases in the programs, teachers and pupils get a narrowed view of what reading is. Figure 2 illustrates this narrowing (Freeman, Y, 1986).

Teachers and pupils get a narrowed view of what reading is.

Figure 2 Narrowing of Text in Basal Readers

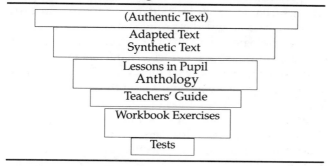

Adapted and Synthetic Texts

The text students read may start out as an authentic text. We've enclosed it in parentheses because it is the exception rather than the rule when the text has not been revised before the pupil reads it in the basal. So the text is narrowed by the process of revision. The revision may involve shortening sentences, substituting more frequent for less frequent words and phrases, using shorter words, simplifying syntax, eliminating or modifying plot features. Or it may be a synthetic text, one produced by the authors and editors of the basals to fit their scope and sequence criteria.

Table 2 shows the kinds of texts used in two basals. Almost all the authentic texts are poems or songs in both series. In some of the early levels, although these appear in the pupils' texts, they are to be read to pupils by the teacher. In some programs other poems appear primarily in the tearchers' manual for reading aloud. Most of the first-grade selections in all series, as in these two, are synthetic. In third and fifth grade most of the selections are adapted; that is, revised, abridged, or both.

It is the exception rather than the rule when the text has not been revised.

For many years the pre-primers and primers used synthetic texts centered around children in a suburban/rural family. Thus Dick and Jane were well-known to Scott, Foresman pupils, while Tom and Betty were familiar to Ginn pupils. That changed when the civil rights and feminist movements questioned the ethnic and gender narrowness in the texts. So a wider range of settings, characters and experiences appeared in early levels of basals, and the primers and pre-primers became anthologies. Harcourt's program, however, maintains a central cast of interracial characters in a vaguely urban setting. Here is what they say: "The preprimers, *Sun Up, Happy Morning,* and *Magic Afternoon* (Levels 1-3) are not anthologies. Instead, each preprimer is a delightful book of related stories about a single group of characters" (Harcourt, Teachers Edition, p. xxiv). Harcourt provides a "bonus" selection at the end of each pupil's book in Levels 1 through 9. These are not accompanied by skill instruction, "for their purpose is to motivate pupils to read independently for pleasure." But in

Table 2   Revised, Synthetic and Authentic Texts

Level	Grade	Number of Texts		Revised or Abridged (in percent)		Synthetic or House Written (in percent)		Authenic
Ginn								
2	1	7	1	14.29	6	85.71	0	0
3	1	10	0	0	9	90.00	1	10
4	1	11	2	18.18	8	72.73	1	9.09
5	1 Primer	29	7	24.14	18	62.07	4	13.79
6	1 First	27	9	33.33	16	59.26	2	7.41
10	3 Part 2	33	21	63.64	8	24.24	4	12.12
12	5	52	33	63.46	11	21.15	8	15.38
Holt								
3	1	12	0	0	11	91.67	1	8.33
4	1	10	0	0	6	60.00	4	40
5	1	8	0	0	6	75.00	2	25
6	1	10	2	20	5	50.00	3	30
7	1 Primer	21	5	23.81	9	42.86	7	33.33
8	1 First	27	7	25.93	11	40.74	9	33.33
11	3	38	17	44.74	11	28.95	10	26.32
12	3	46	21	45.65	11	23.91	14	30.43
14	5	80	25	31.25	31	38.75	24	30

the pre-primers they are "brief stories written especially for HBJ." In later levels they are revised versions of "previously published children's stories."

The reason that so little in the basals is authentic language and so much is synthetic or revised, is that the focus on words and skills commits publishers to control the language of what pupils read. Harcourt, like the other basal publishers, says that keeping language natural is important, but they seem to feel that it can be both natural and controlled. This statement appears in the front matter of the teachers' edition:

> In HBJ *Bookmark, Eagle Edition,* the basal vocabulary—the number of different words that appear in the Pupil's Edition—is realistic, and the rate of word recurrence is unusually high. A concentrated effort is made to keep the language in the Pupil's Editions as natural as possible. The controlled rate of word introduction, the frequent recurrence of words, and the natural language, combined with the close relationship between new words and known phonics elements, result in a treatment of vocabulary that is managed easily by most children (Harcourt, Teacher's Edition).

Here is how Gerald McDermott, an award-winning children's author begins his retelling of the Japanese folktale he calls *The Stonecutter:*

> Tasuko was a lowly stonecutter. Each day the sound of his hammer and chisel rang out as he chipped away at the foot of the mountain. He hewed the blocks of stone that formed the great temples and palaces.
>
> He asked for nothing more than to work each day, and this pleased the spirit who lived in the mountains (McDermott, 1975).

Here's the beginning of Harcourt's retelling of the same folktale:

Once there was a strong man. Each morning he went to the mountain. There he dug up stones. He broke them into pebbles with a large steel hammer. He carried the pebbles to the village,
where he sold them

(Harcourt, Level 8, Grade 3).

The reason that so little in the basals is authentic language and so much is synthetic or revised, is that the focus on words and skills commits publishers to control the language of what pupils read.

Pupils will rarely meet the language of any children's author in a pure and unadapted form.

Harcourt's editors do not seem to have been able to follow all of their control criteria and at the same time create a natural text. Meaning is also changed. In McDermott's telling the stonecutter's wishes to be transformed into more and more powerful entities are heard and granted by the spirit of the mountains. In Harcourt's retelling he gets his wishes with no apparent help.

The claims of basal publishers that they draw on the available rich literature for children is certainly true. But it is also true that pupils will rarely meet the language of any children's author in a pure and unadapted form.

In Freeman's study of Spanish basals she found it was also likely that the text would have been translated from English. In fact, one program is a verbatim translation of an English-language basal from the same company that publishes the Spanish-language version.

Fractured Language

As we have seen the language of basal texts is further narrowed and reduced in the teachers' guide, workbook exercises, and skill sheets. Here the reader is often dealing with letters, word parts, words, phrases, sentence fragments and sets of unrelated sentences. The stories that are included are synthetic, short, and lacking in cohesion.

For example an exercise in the Harcourt teachers' manual, immediately preceding the selection above, involves variant sounds of *e*. The teacher is told to write the word *bed* on the chalkboard. Then pupils are to raise their hands to indicate which word in pairs of words the teacher says aloud has the same vowel sound. The pairs are:

break, bend   sheep, shell
next, new   feast, fence

The exercise is then repeated for several other sounds. Following that, a workbook page is provided. It has two parts. In the first the pupils are given lists of three words and asked to underline which two have the same vowel sounds. In the second part they must chose one of three words to fit a blank in a short sentence:

Both students and teachers will naturally assume that what is tested is what is important.

---

1. The water pipes are _____ the ground.
below   became   become

In fine print it is indicated that the objective is relating sounds to letters and identifying words using context and variant sounds with e.

Then an exercise requires pupils to match the phrases a *tall* mountain, a quiet *village* with sentence stems. The prefix un- and suffixes -ly, -er, and -est are introduced in a brief exercise. Next new words, *pebbles* and *suddenly,* are explicitly introduced. The teacher is also told that the other new words in the following story are broke, stones, matter, sold, *indoors,* but that pupils "should be able to decode them independently, using skills they have learned in this program."

The promise of this pre-reading activity is that it will help pupils to read the story. But isolating elements from a text makes them abstractions: words and word parts. It also continues the implication for learners, particularly when the text is inauthentic and somewhat strange sounding, that the important thing is to learn the words and skills and the story is only practice for doing that.

What's Tested

The final narrowing takes place in the tests. Both students and teachers will naturally assume that what is tested is what is important. What's tested is broadly what the program teaches, but not everything in the program is as easily tested in the usual multiple-choice format of basal tests.

In the tests accompanying six first-grade programs from two-thirds to four-fifths of the test items involve word identification. For purposes of comparison the figures include both phonics and vocabulary items. All programs have both, but the terms they use for the sub-tests vary. A high proportion of the Economy items are specifically labeled phonics. In third-grade tests 40 to 70 percent, in the programs we examined, dealt with word identification. The fifth-grade tests we examined varied in emphasis on word identification. Scott, Foresman emphasized less than 10 percent. The programs vary, then, in how much word identification continues to dominate in the upper grades.

In the Harcourt program, for Level 8 (second grade), the cumulative test has this item breakdown:

Vocabulary, 16 questions (18 percent)
Word service/Decoding, 31 questions (36 percent)
Comprehension, 16 questions (18 percent). This is broken down into: Main ideas, 2 questions, Finding pronoun antecedents 4 questions,
Making judgments, 2 questions
Distinguishing fact and opinion, 8 questions
Language Skills, 12 questions (14 percent) of which 8 are recognizing contractions and 4 are using suffixes to identify words.

Thus only 18 percent of the cumulative test questions for the level are intended to test comprehension. Here's what those questions look like:

Read each story. Then fill in the circle next to the sentence that tells the main idea of each story.

1. When Ruth started to ride her bicycle, she heard a loud pop. Her back tire was flat! Ruth got her tools and took off the back wheel. She fixed the flat and put the tire back on the wheel. Then she finished her ride.

( ) Ruth heard a loud pop.
( ) Ruth fixed the flat tire.
( ) Ruth used her tools.

2. Last summer Pete got on a ship for a trip to Alaska. On the ship he saw beautiful sights. The ship sailed close to the shore of Canada. Pete saw quiet, green forests and snow-covered mountains. He also watched the pink sun set over the ocean.

( ) The pink sun set over the ocean.
( ) The ship sailed near the shore.
( ) Pete saw beautiful sights.

(HBJ, Level 8 Cumulative Test)

The pupils have had similar experiences in the program picking a main idea for a short one-paragraph "story." So they may be able to decide which of the choices provided the item-writer would consider correct. But neither the score on the whole test or the score on the portion labeled comprehension are testing the reader's ability to comprehend natural language texts. Rather what is being tested is the ability of pupils to successfully respond to "skill items," including comprehension "skills." That fits the logic of the program and the evaluation logic that tests should be "objective-referenced"; that is, they should measure pupils' ability to do what the program teaches.

In one unit test for Ginn's level 9 (third grade, the same level as "Alvin's Masterpiece") there are 12 decoding questions (29 percent), 17 vocabulary questions (40 percent), 9 comprehension questions (19 percent), and 4 life skill questions (10 percent). So only 19 percent of the items are intended to test comprehension. Life skills here means reading symbols and signs.

Some examples of the comprehension items are:

Judy is trying to sell lemonade. She has set up a table outside her house. The sign says, "Lemonade for sale." A man

Only 18 percent of the cumulative test questions for the level are intended to test comprehension.

walks by and reads the sign. Then he says, "I am really thirsty."

3. What will happen next?
   a. The man will buy the sign.
   b. Judy will take the lemonade inside.
   c. The man will buy some lemonade.

Wilbur wants to write a story. He closes the door of his room. Then he sits down at his desk. He gets some paper out of his notebook. Then he picks up his pencil.

5. What will happen next?
   a. Wilbur will draw on the door.
   b. Wilbur will leave the room.
   c. Wilbur will start writing the story.

It appears that the item-writers were trying to test pupils' ability to deal with cause and effect or predict outcomes, two kinds of comprehension "skills" in Ginn's program. What they have produced are short, unnatural texts which are less interesting, less natural, and less predictable than the stories in the pupils' anthology. Here's how "Alvin's Masterpiece" begins:

Alvin Artwork just loved to paint. I suppose it had to do with his name. He had a strange way of painting though. Splat! The paint would fly onto his art paper

(Ginn, Level 9, p. 224).

The synthetic language of the tests is much reduced from the kind of language the story in the book presents. To produce correct answers the pupils must accept such test items as a special form of language and then deal with the pragmatics of a situation in which none of the answers are wrong but only one of them is right. They must learn what Bloome has called procedural display, a way of responding acceptably to teachers and school situations (Bloome, Puro, and Theodorou, in press). To be credited with good comprehension the pupil must be able to identify which response the testmaker is most likely to approve. Such items only comprise 18 percent of the Harcourt test and

19 percent of the Ginn test. The rest involves even less language than these.

The Poor Get Poorer

This narrowing from authentic text to virtual non-text has an ironic side effect. Those pupils who are seen as doing well in the basal program gradually experience, within the program, more complete and interesting texts. They are likely to be encouraged to read outside of the program in a range of real books written for children. Those who are seen as less successful will get less exposure to meaningful language and more drill and practice materials with reduced language or non-texts. And they are likely to be discouraged from attempting to read real books. In fact almost the only suggestion the basals offer for pupils who are not succeeding in the program is additional practice.

WHERE IS MEANING?

Scholars and researchers have argued over the centuries the issue of where meaning is in language. A growing multidisciplinary consensus supports the view that meaning emerges from a transaction between the reader and the text (Purvis, 1984). The text, if it is a cohesive natural text, has a meaning potential. The reader brings to the reading a life view, a set of values, and a set of schemas built through experience in a large number of language events. So meaning is constructed during reading. It results from the transaction with the text and is as much dependent on the reader as on the author and the text.

The makers of basals are not unaware of this emerging consensus that meaning is constructed by each reader during reading. That's reflected in the articles in the teachers' manuals by program authors or other well-known researchers and authorities. Here, for example, is an excerpt from an article that appears in

Meaning emerges from a transaction between the reader and the text

The focus on single-answer questions during reading makes meaning arbitrary and the same for all readers.

Scott, Foresman's *Focus* series:

> By using clues offered by the text as well as his or her background knowledge, the reader develops an account that may include an understanding of when things are happening, why they are happening and some implications. The reader's comprehension is more than a listing of separate skills or facts; it involves an integration of details, inferences, cause and effect relationships, and other skills. Also, readers enlist numerous behaviors while developing understanding. These include self-questioning, self-correcting, visualizing, interconnecting ideas, analyzing and responding to ideas. (Tierney, 1985)

But the focus in basals on words and skills results in the overwhelming treatment of meaning primarily as a property of words. The focus on single-answer questions during reading makes meaning arbitrary (the text is always right) and the same for all readers. Meaning results, the basals repeatedly demonstrate, from the application of skills in a precise manner. Here for example is a fifth-grade exercise:

---

3. Clues to Word Meaning

Sound-Letter Relationships Sometimes you may come across a word you think you don't know. But if you pronounce it, you may find that it is a word you have heard before. You can use what you know about letter-sound relationships to pronounce such words. It often helps to sound out each syllable. Remember, a **syllable** is a word part that has one vowel sound. The word *octopus* has three syllables (oc-to-pus).

Practice Exercise Use what you know about sound-letter relationships to pronounce each boldfaced word below. Write in the blank the number of syllables in the boldfaced word. Then fill in the circle next to the correct meaning of the word. Use the Answer Key to check your answers.

1. No one knows the number of stars in the whole **universe.**

   a. everything that exists
   b. the sky during the day
   c. planets we can see

2. At the **dairy** we bought butter, cheese, and cream.

   a. a market that sells vegetables
   b. a shop that sells sweet foods
   c. a store that sells foods made of milk

3. Justino Diaz gave an enjoyable **performance** in the opera.

   a. ticket to a play
   b. a brightly colored costume
   c. act of playing a role

4. Who **invented** the telephone?

   a. talked a long time
   b. thought up for the first time
   c. took apart slowly

(HBJ, Level 11, Grade 5)

The logic of this exercise is that by sounding out the syllables of words which don't look familiar, the reader will recognize their sounds and then be able to pick out their meanings. Meanings thus appear to be viewed as the property of known oral words. No attempt is made in such exercises to assure that the assumed conditions of the premise are met; that is, that the particular fifth-grade pupils have these words in their oral vocabularies but do not recognize their written form. The meanings are also assumed to be constant across subjects, or at least the pupils are expected to make their meanings correspond to the item-writer's. But a farm child might have some trouble with the possible meanings of *dairy* provided by the exercise . How many syllables (by the definition) are in *dairy*? In fact, how would a pupil know how many syllables are in the word unless the pupil knew what the word was? Consider, for example, that the similar word, diary, has three syllables.

ISOLATING LANGUAGE FROM ITS USE

Many scholars over the centuries have commented on functions of language; that is, what people use language for. Halliday (1985) concluded from a longitudinal language study that children learn language at the same time that they use language to learn. The development of uses for language is what stimulates natural

Pupils are given little choice about what they will or won't read.

language development. It is the need to use language to communicate that motivates language development. What this means is that language (reading and writing included) is learned most easily when it is functional. That creates a major problem for basal readers. Little of the material pupils are asked to read in basals is functional for them. Meaningful stories come closest since one function of reading is the pleasure that comes from an interesting story; but the stories in the basals may or may not be of interest to any particular pupil. Furthermore, as we have seen, the basic function of the stories in the basal is to provide practice for vocabulary and skills. That's why they are revised to suit the skill sequence and the controlled vocabulary, and why the reading is repeatedly interrupted. Pupils are given little choice about what they will or won't read.

Expository material can also be functional if readers are reading to get information. However, when such material occurs in the basals the function and particular purpose is almost always an assigned one, and the pupil may again see only an instructional function and not a personal one. To a certain extent, the problem of lack of functionality and purpose for the particular learner could be ameliorated by paying more attention to building on the personal needs, interests, and motivations of the learners; and certainly that's what many teachers do as they use basals. But the basal manuals do little to facilitate this personalization of the programs; and the controlled nature of many of the selections makes it difficult. Often pupils are asked during reading to predict what will happen next. But their predictions are judged by how closely they conform to a literally interpreted text.

The manuals frequently indicate that editors and authors are concerned with providing a full range of language genres so that pupils may experience a full range of language functions. Houghton Mifflin says it represents every type and style of selection: fiction, nonfiction, poetry, exposition, personal narratives, biography, folktales, fairy tales, as well as content reading in social studies, science, and the arts. In a study of eight basal programs researchers found, however, that there is not a full representation of kinds of language in basals (Flood and Lapp, 1987).

In order to control and sequence language it is isolated from its normal personal-social use.

> Our inspection shows that basals are predominantly literary, with 65 percent of the selections and 72 percent of the pages containing either narratives or poems. Furthermore, we could not find in the basal manuals one consistent approach for guiding teachers in designing instruction for the different kinds of writing included in the readers. The procedures recommended were not significantly different than those recommended for most narrative stories. This is unfortunate, because there is a good deal of research indicating that instruction in reading expository texts should be approached differently from narrative texts if the interaction between the reader and the text is to be successful (Flood and Lapp, p. 302-304).

In any case, all this according to one publisher has the purpose of "enabling students to learn and practice skills they'll need across the whole curriculum" (Houghton Mifflin, Teacher's Notebook p. 9).

In order to control and sequence language it is isolated from its normal personal-social use. It is true that there are suggestions in basals which encourage pupils to select books to read on their own. There are suggestions for pupils to seek the answers for their own questions by finding informational materials that may have the answers. But these are enrichments to be used after the skills and the words have been attended to.

CONTROLLING LEARNING

If the basal reader is to be a complete technology for developing reading that will be successful for all learners regardless of any differences among them, then the basal must assume a view of learning that makes it possible to control the learning with carefully planned and controlled acts of teaching which each result in an act of learning. This view is carefully expounded in the teachers' guide and represented in the lesson structures, the revisions of the reading selections to support skill instruction, and the equation of scores on basal tests with reading development.

Building on the Laws of Learning

Our examination shows that today, as in their inception, basal readers use a view of learning rooted in Thorndyke's *Laws of Learning.* The *Law of Readiness* results in the readiness materials and in the tight sequence in which skill is built upon skill. The *Law of Exercise* produces drills and exercises in pupil books, workbooks, and supplemental materials. The *Law of Effect* supports the sequence of first learning words and skills and then using them in reading selections; and the *Law of Identical Elements* results in the focus on isolated skills in testing for development of reading ability and for the close match between the items in the exercises and the tests.

Harcourt says in their program: "Relevant skills are taught and practiced before pupils need those skills in reading a selection"(Harcourt, Level 8, 1983, p xxiv).

Scott, Foresman uses what it calls "effective and efficient four-step teaching." These steps are:

1. Teach—pupils are taught skills before they are expected to use them.
2. Practice—There is immediate follow-up on what is taught.
3. Apply—What has been practiced is then applied in real reading. Retention is likely because it comes right after teaching and practice.
4. Assess—So re-teaching can take place if needed.

Three extra steps provide, in Scott, Foresman's view, for individualization:

5. Reteach
6. Reinforce
7. Enrich

Passive, Controlled Learners

In this view learning is the result of teaching, piece by piece, item by item. The whole, reading, is the sum of the parts, words and skills. Learners are passive and controlled.

The authors and editors of basals seem to be aware that this passive, controlled role for the learner has its problems. Here's an excerpt from an abridged article included in a Holt teachers' guide:

> When...I made a pest of myself interrupting to correct errors, the children made it quite clear that they did not appreciate my meddling....On the other hand, in the role of attentive, non-critical listener, I found it nearly impossible to stop them from reading to me. And in no instance did any miscue that distorted the sense of the message go uncorrected, or at least undetected by the children themselves (Mayer, 1976 reprinted in Holt, Level 11 Teachers' Guide).

Basal manuals indicate attempts to achieve less passive roles for learners. Houghton Mifflin attempts in its program to develop metacognition in young pupils' learning to read. It quotes researchers:

> ...metacognition refers to going beyond thinking to the point of understanding how thinking and learning take place (Brown, 1980). With conscious understanding of a complex cognitive process comes greater ability to use that process correctly and consistently. Through metacognitive development, students learn which strategies are needed to complete a task successfully; they are able to determine whether or not they are performing tasks correctly (Comprehension Monitoring) and they learn how to apply strategies for making needed corrections
>
> (Calfee and Piontowski, 1981 quoted in Houghton Mifflin, Note Book Section 11, pp. 37-38).

But Houghton Mifflin is committed to "empirically validated procedures for directly teaching the skills that improve comprehension" (p. 40). How does one directly teach metacognition as a skill to improve comprehension? As early as Level B (first pre-primer) children are assumed to be showing metacognition by

In this view learning is the result of teaching, piece by piece, item by item. Learners are passive and controlled.

The view that learning must be controlled, which is built into the basal, takes metacognition, a property of the learner, and makes it a property of the program.

responding to the teachers' questions. By Level F their metacognition is built directly by getting them to put their recollections of the skills they have been taught into their own words in response to questions such as: "What will thinking about the things that happened in the story help you to do?" Or "When you read a story, why should you think about what might happen next?" (Houghton Mifflin, Level F, *Bells*, Teachers' Guide, p. 13).

Again, there is the assumption that the way to teach something is to get students to respond to questions with acceptable answers. Are pupils learning to think about cognitive processes and thereby understand them (metacognition)? Or are they learning how to answer questions about what they are supposed to think? Metacognition may, indeed, facilitate comprehension. But is it a teachable prerequisite to comprehension, or something that develops like cognition itself in the active pursuit of knowledge? The view that learning must be controlled, which is built into the basal, takes metacognition, a property of the learner, and makes it a property of the program.

CONTROLLING TEACHING

We've documented the fact that basals began in an era in which teachers had minimal professional education. So one of the goals of basals was to provide explicit controls for sub-professional teachers. Furthermore the application of the Laws of Learning led to basals closely equating acts of learning with acts of teaching. In that view controlling learning depends on controlling teaching. That's what the basal manuals are still organized to do.

Have pupils open their books to page 12-13. Read the title on page 13 aloud. Then ask pupils to read the paragraphs silently to find out what the boy in the picture is trying to do

(Scott, Foresman, *Focus*, Up and Over, Teachers' Edition, Level 7, grade 3-1, p. 5).

That's how one publisher addresses the teacher. The verbs are imperatives; the procedure is highly specific and invariant. Pupils may feel that the teacher is in control, but in fact it is the basal which is in control. The purpose for the reading is set not by the learner or the teacher but by the basal. This example is not unique but typical of basals.

The purpose for the reading is set not by the learner or the teacher but by the basal.

Display the words *trick* and *truck* for the children to compare. Note that the u̲ has the vowel sound heard in c̲u̲p̲. Have them complete this sentence. *The farmer drives a* _____ *(truck).* Then display the word *trucks* below *truck.* Have the children note the difference between the two words and read the sentences:
I see the trucks. Can you see the trucks?

(Holt, A Place for Me, Level 7, Primer, Teachers' Edition, T-10).

This script is provided by Holt. It appears under a heading, "Developing Vocabulary." It's designed for the use of first-grade teachers. One might think that this specificity results from the need the basal developers feel to carefully control skill and word introduction in the beginning year of reading instruction. But the specificity and the tightness of the control does not ease as pupils become more advanced.

Here's an example from a fifth grade basal:

[The following appears in red print indicating that it is a script the teacher is to follow]:

What is a prefix? (A prefix is an addition to the beginning of a word that changes or extends the meaning of the word.)

What prefixes are written on the chart? (The prefixes on the chart are *un, dis, re.*)

What words can you make by combining the prefixes with the words on the chart? (Answers may vary but may include uncover, unlock, untie, discover, disarm, disclose, disqualify, dislocate, discharge, recover, rearm, relocate, and recharge).

[Now the print shifts to black indicating instructions for the teacher to follow]. Write the words on the chalkboard as the students volunteer them.

(Economy, Uncharted Waters, Level M, Grade 5, p. 48).

The view of the teacher incorporated by the basal is that of a scripted technician faithfully following the detailed lessons provided with the basal.

Scripts are also provided to deal with comprehension. Here's one from another fifth-grade teachers' edition. In this series the scripted part is in italics and the instructions for the teacher to follow are in standard print:

Remind students that characters in a story or poem can have the same feelings they do. Explain that writers help readers understand how characters feel by telling what characters do or say. Direct students to the top of page 120. *How does Lila feel when she hangs up the phone?* (Disappointed, sorry for herself) *How did the writer help you know?* (She wrote that   Lila sighed and muttered, "Happy nothingday to me.")

(Macmillan, *Reading Express, Bold Dreams,* Teachers' Edition, Level 11, Grade 5, p 134)

There are also scripts for study skills, such as the following:

Remind students that when they follow directions, they should pay attention to the steps so that what they make will turn out right. Read aloud the following paragraphs and have students check the selection to determine their answers.

Susan wanted to make a shell mobile like the one described on page 196. She used heavy thread to hang shells from a bar of driftwood. When she tied the mobile to a hook it leaned to one side. What detail of the directions did Susan forget to follow? (She forgot to balance the mobile)

(Harcourt Brace Jovanovich, *Blazing Trails,* Level 11,
Grade 5, Teachers' Edition, p. T160).

Teachers as Scripted Technicians in the Basal Program

There are many roles that teachers can and do perform in their classrooms. The view of the teacher incorporated by the basal is that of a scripted technician faithfully following the detailed lessons provided with the basal. The program itself does the teaching as long as the teacher does and says what the teachers' manual says to do.

There are some advantages to the teacher in accepting the role of scripted technician. The teacher needs to do little planning other than reviewing the manual to make sure that the right components are available at the time they are needed. The workbooks, skill sheets, and other materials keep pupils occupied in what the manual says are necessary activities. Pupils appear to be "on task." Also, the teacher need not learn more about the teaching and learning of reading since all that is handled by the program. Most important, by following the manuals diligently, accepting the premise that the experts who wrote it must know what they are doing, the teacher need feel neither responsibility nor guilt if some pupils are unsuccessful. The teacher role assigned by the basal is a relatively safe refuge for teachers, particularly those with self-doubts or for the teacher under pressure from administrators for assured results on standardized tests.

If treating the teacher as a scripted technician in the manuals were only a matter of phrasing and in fact teachers generally used professional judgments in how they used the basals it would not be so important. But Shannon, as reported earlier, found that teachers are generally required to follow the basals closely and that they are likely to follow them anyway even when not required to do so, because they believe the basals are scientific. Furthermore, it is not easy for a teacher to steer a middle course, following the basals but modifying the instructional sequence and procedures. Duffy, Roehler, and Putnam (1987) found, in a study in which they attempted to help teachers make more effective use of basals, that "there are no easily identifiable patterns that teachers could use to modify either the content or the instructional design of what the 'master developers' prescribed in the basal. As one of our teachers said, `You can't understand it; you can only follow it'"(p. 362).

The dominant view built into the basal, lesson by lesson, is that teaching is a sequence of telling and/or modeling, drilling, and questioning.

Pedagogical Approach

There is, as there always has been, eclecticism in the basals' pedagogy, their approach to instruction. But the dominant view built into the basal, lesson by lesson, is that teaching is a sequence of telling and/or modeling, drilling, and questioning. This has not changed, but phrasing has changed to pick up the catchwords of the profession in a given period.

> The total skills program offers sufficient repetition of instruction and practice to aid in achieving mastery. Varied teaching strategies include modeling, direct instruction and direct practice.
>
> (Macmillan, p. T10)

The pedagogy requires that there be a sequence of relatively specific "learnings" for each lesson to focus on. The source of these has normally been some kind of breaking down of the act of reading into skill and sub-skill components. Defining reading as being able to recognize or attack words has generally given a means of organizing teaching lessons around sequences of word-attack skills and controlled vocabulary. It also provides for immediately measurable results, since each lesson focuses on specific "skills" or "words."

This pedagogy is present in all the basals, whether they claim to be phonics or word-centered and whether they are aimed at a general population, a remedial population, or an Hispanic population.

There is an intrinsic appeal and logic to a view that says to teach something you break it down into its components and teach it one piece at a time, making sure each piece is mastered, until the learner is fully knowledgeable. It also has great appeal to those who want to be able to measure learning per unit of time or money spent to achieve learning.

THE BASAL TESTS

The logic of the basal technology and the actual design of the basals result in tests becoming the essence of the programs. The logic is that if basals are followed diligently the pupils will learn to read and that achievement is directly reflected in performance on the tests. Teachers and administrators will put their heaviest emphasis on the aspects of the programs that are tested and spend less time on those elements that are not.

With strong acceptance of the basals in American reading programs, the tests that publishers provide come to play a major role in the school life of most pupils. In fact, it may well be that more vital decisions are made in American schools on the basis of tests in the basal reading programs than on the basis of any other tests, including achievement tests. Decisions are made on placement and assignment to ability groups for reading instruction, and on progress from level to level. But decisions are also made about organizing schools and placement of students in classrooms using the basal tests to limit the ability range in each class. Decisions are made about promotion and retention on the assumption that reading is the key to achievement and that basal tests precisely measure progress in reading. Decisions are even made about the effectiveness of teachers and schools on the basis of their pupils basal test scores.

Harcourt Brace calls its periodic tests "an instructional management system designed to help you make short-term assessments of each pupil's progress in reading. They can also help you diagnose each pupil's skill needs and prescribe appropriate instruction to meet those needs." Though the phrasing is careful, the use of both industrial management and clinical medical terminology strongly evokes a sense of precise, effective, scientific control. So it is not hard to understand why schools place such importance on performance on basal tests.

Ginn says:

> The results of the Level Test help teachers decide whether a pupil should proceed to the next level, whether additional help is needed if the pupil does

Decisions are also made about organizing schools and placement of students in classrooms using the basal tests to limit the ability range in each class.

proceed, or whether reteaching is needed before the pupil proceeds to the next level. Although Level Tests function primarily as survey instruments, they may also be used diagnostically.

...The tested objectives within each level were selected because they are considered essential preparation for the objectives of the following level as well as being necessary for the long-range goal of achieving general reading competency.

Again the wording is careful; the results help teachers decide. But the implication is a strong one: Reading is precisely measured by the tests and poor performance at one level means the learner lacks preparation not only for the next level but for "achieving general reading competency."

With such strong claims being made for the tests, they deserve careful consideration in this report.

Test Components

Each reading series we reviewed is accompanied by a set of tests. There is variation in the arrangement of testing procedures for different series. Some have alternate forms of tests to facilitate pre-testing and post-testing. Some have unit tests and level tests. Some have unit tests within level tests. Most have placement tests. All incorporate a version of level testing; that is, testing for each book read in the series. Within the tests of each of the programs the focus is usually broken down into three basic parts:

1. some sort of word analysis or word study component variously named decoding (Economy, Ginn, HBJ); word identification (Scott, Foresman), vocabulary (Economy, Ginn, HBJ) , sounds and letters/decoding (Holt); or word service (HBJ)
2. a comprehension component
3. a study, life and/or language skills component.

These parallel the programs themselves.

**Figure 2.
First-grade Basal
Reader Test
Summary**

**Figure 3.
Third-grade Basal
Test Summary**

**Figure 4.
Fifth-grade Basal
Test Summary**

Reading is not making sense of print any more. It is doing well on the basal tests.

Figures 2 to 4 show the proportion of test items devoted to these categories in several basal tests in grades 1, 3, and 5. These figures use the publishers own categorizations. Our study showed that the items do not always appear to be testing what they say they test.

Figure 2 shows that in tests for six programs the greatest emphasis in grade one is on the decoding/vocabulary components which are sometimes separated and sometimes combined. If the vocabulary and decoding strands are added to create a general category of word identification/attack, as in the Scott, Foresman program, the programs are almost identical for grade one with a high emphasis on word aspects as opposed to comprehension.

The trend across programs for grade three is a lessening emphasis on the word or sub-word aspect and an increase in testing for study/research skills and comprehension (*see* Figure 3). This trend continues into grade five to the point where the decoding category almost disappears and is either replaced by a vocabulary emphasis (as in Economy) or by a diffused emphasis on the remaining categories (*see* Figure 4). Ginn and Holt are exceptions to this trend since they maintain the decoding strand into grade five.

Reductionism and Reification

Figures 2-4 demonstrate that reading ability is reduced, as it is evaluated, to some skills which are considered components of skilled reading. In philosophy this tendency to reduce any reality to a few of its conditions is called *reductionism*. Having reduced the reality of reading to measuring some of what is taught in the rest of the program, this reduced reality is then reified; that is, treated as the reality itself. So reading is not making sense of print any more. It is doing well on the basal tests.

Amount of Testing

Given the composition of basal readers, with several levels comprising first-grade, it is not surprising that the greatest number of tests possible for any one grade usually occurs at grade one. If placement test items are excluded, and children were given pre- and post-tests, as well as level tests, they might complete anywhere from approximately 256 items (Scott, Foresman) to 1,578 (Economy) items across the span of the grade-one school year. It appears that, if all tests are used, it is possible for a first-grade student to complete more than six times as many items as a fifth-grade student.

Stated Purposes

We indicated above some of the things publishers say about how their tests can be used. Most differentiate the use of unit tests, completed after each sequence of lessons, and level tests, completed as each book is finished.

Macmillan says:

> ...the Unit Test scores are designed to be reported by objective and skill area to provide one indication of the student's general reading performance.

Here is the reification; Test scores indicate reading performance.

Ginn says:

> Unit tests assess pupil achievement on the critical instructional objectives in each unit. Not all objectives in a unit are tested....An objective is tested only after pupils have had at least three instructional exposures to it.

> They are not designed, as are standardized tests, to encourage comparison of one pupil with another or with a nationwide norm group. Nor are they designed to rank-order pupils on an achievement scale, yielding a distribution of scores from low to high in the form of the familiar "bell-shaped curve." Because pupils are being tested only on material they have been taught

These tests are not diagnostic, since that would imply that they are tied directly to some model of reading competence, which they are not.

and only after several practices, their scores may be near perfect, especially on the Decoding and Vocabulary strands. Therefore, high scores on Unit Tests are to be expected.

Level tests—Harcourt calls them cumulative tests— are used to measure achievement of the objectives of the levels and are therefore more likely to be involved in long-term important decisions by teachers and school authorities.

Classifying Basal Tests

Certain terms recur throughout the publishers' descriptions of their tests:

diagnostic—Economy, HBJ, Ginn
mastery—Economy, Macmillan
competence—HBJ, Ginn
criterion-referenced—MacMillan, HBJ

The intent of the test makers is to create a test which evaluates important elements of what is included in the particular reading program. Some of these quotations above explicitly make reference to such an intent, while in others the intent is implied. So these tests fall, as a group, into the criterion-referenced or objective-referenced types of assessment. These tests are not diagnostic, since that would imply that they are tied directly to some model of reading competence, which they are not.

Conformity to Psychometric Standards

Popham (1981) states that objective-based tests, which are constructed to measure an instructional objective and are similar to behavioral objectives, do not "supply the degree of descriptive detail necessary to tie down satisfactorily just what it is that an examinee's test performance really means" (p. 29). Crocker and Algina (1986) state that the development of a criterion-referenced test "begins with a set of instructional objectives and then proceeds to define a domain of performance to which inferences from test scores will be made" (p. 69).

According to Popham (1981) "a criterion referenced test is used to ascertain an individual's status with respect to a defined behavioral domain" (p. 27). This definition has several components each of which must be considered for appropriate application. First of all there is the question of the specification of the behavioral domain, and second there is the issue of what the criterion is, since it is the criterion which is the gauge of the test.

Bormuth (1970) claims that "the concepts and procedures traditionally employed in the construction of achievement test items are defined wholly in the private subjective life of the test writer, which makes achievement testing little better than a dark art" (pp. 2-3). Perhaps in reaction to such critical statements by researchers procedures for item generation are now specified in measurement texts. Generally, the procedure recommended is to set up test specifications which will form the basis for the item generation procedure. Popham (1978) indicated that setting out the specifications of a test enables test-users to identify what it is the test is measuring, and enables test-writers to create pools of items which measure a behavior in exactly the same manner.

Crocker and Algina (1986) suggest a table of specifications as one means of managing the test specifications generated. A table of specifications is simply a two-way grid with cognitive processes on one axis and content areas on the other. The number in the cell at which these dimensions intersect is an arbitrary value that the examiner chooses, which determines how much emphasis will be given to that area in this test. Despite this attempted objectivity in item development, Wardrop, Anderson, Hively, Hastings, Anderson and Muller (1982) note that even with a table of specifications, or list of objectives, "there are seldom explicit

Questions of validity and reliability seem to be bypassed by test-writers.

rules for generating items from each such objective" (p. 5).

Given the relatively embryonic state of measurement technology with respect to criterion-referenced and objective-referenced assessment, how do the basal reader tests fare? First of all, in most cases the teachers' manual accompanying the tests is nothing more than a script for administering the tests. Although in a number of programs objectives are cross-referenced to pages in the teachers' edition which contain related lessons, reteaching activities, reteaching practice, and workbook pages, tables of specifications have not been provided.

With respect to validity and reliability Macmillan states that field-testing, verification, and validation of *Reading Express* were conducted by National Evaluation Systems in Maine. However, apart from this reference, questions of validity and reliability seem to be bypassed by test-writers.

There is a key problem in field-testing objective referenced tests. The tests are, at least in principle, designed to evaluate what the programs teach. But they must be available at the time that the program is published. The only students who could fairly be assessed with the tests are those who have completed the related portion of the program, unit, or level. But at the time of publication no students have completed the program. The only ways to avoid this problem would be to delay development and publication of the tests until there are pupils available who have completed the program, or to conduct elaborate and extensive field-testing of each unit and level before the program is actually published. We could discover no evidence that any publishers of tests we examined had done either.

Scoring

The selection of a value that constitutes mastery is an

arbitrary one in this kind of assessment. Popham (1978) has suggested several strategies upon which to base the performance standard for an assessment device. However, in none of the tests examined was any rationale provided for the selection of the particular cut-off points used.

Of those we considered the Economy and Holt tests were the most consistent. Economy tests had a narrow range of 80 to 86 percent with most sub-tests falling at 80 percent competency levels. In the Holt tests the range was a little wider with most competency ratings falling in the 67 percent to 76 percent range. The remainder fall at 67 percent minimum competency level. Economy test publishers recommend that "each sub-test should be scored and interpreted separately," and state that "the scores are then grouped to indicate whether a student has competency in a skill or needs reteaching in a skill."

For the HBJ series the stated criterion in the test manual is 80 percent or higher for periodic tests, while the actual range is from 75 to 100 percent. On the Cumulative tests an 80 to 88 percent range constitutes the passing criterion.

In the Ginn program suggested passing scores range from 78 percent to 82 percent for Level test totals, 74 percent to 86 percent for Level sub-test Totals, and 66 percent to 86 percent for Level sub-subtest totals. For Unit tests suggested passing scores range from 75 percent to 83 percent of items in a category.

The question of passing scores relates to the number of items tested for a skill and the relative importance of that skill to reading. For instance, in one of the Economy tests each specific concept or skill was tested with five or six items, thereby giving all skills equal weighting. In the Ginn and Holt programs some skills had only three items. Issues such as the length of the test and the number of items relate to the unaddressed issues of reliability and validity. Where different numbers of items are assigned to different objectives there is

There is no evidence, in their design or in their apparent development, that they meet theoretical criteria for the type of testing they represent.

a resultant variable weighting for the objectives. We could not find rationales for such weighting.

A second aspect of the passing score that must be considered is its relation to mastery of the reading level as a whole. As noted, in the Economy series teachers are advised to examine each sub-test individually and to look at grouped scores later. Minimum competency scores are not given for these grouped scores. In the Ginn and HBJ programs competency scores are given for sub-tests, sub-test groups, and for the total.

To accommodate mastery testing Ginn, Economy, HBJ, and Macmillan all have alternate forms. The issue of equivalence of the forms is not dealt with by publishers. In addition, the equivalence of forms is a moot point if forms fail to have validity or reliability.

What we can conclude from this examination of the basal tests is that there is no evidence, in their design or in their apparent development, that they meet theoretical criteria for the type of testing they represent (if it can be said that they represent any). They are intended to evaluate pupils' success with components of the programs. They provide no evidence that they have evaluated pupil success, that in fact the tests are not simply arbitrary sets of questions labeled to conform to the program objective label. There is no evidence that the minimal passing scores are not simply arbitrary.

Execution—A Validity Related Issue

One way the tests used in basals can be examined is to take at face value the claims of what that is intended to do and see how they are carried through. In other words, given that the test designers specified reading is to be assessed in a specific manner, how well did those designers carry out what they intended?

We stayed at a relatively surface level of our examination of the tests. Had we gone more deeply into each aspect we would have raised a whole new level of concern about the execution of the tests.

Based upon the item-by-item analysis of sets of one form of the test for each of a number of series, several broad descriptive criticisms may be made about the execution problems in the tests that accompany basal readers under review.

1. **Right answers for wrong reasons.** For all series there were items on tests where a student could have achieved success through means other than the stated objective. In some instances items could be successfully completed using common knowledge without even reading the text.

   In addition, problems occurred in targeting a letter for assessment of phonic knowledge or in assessing vocabulary. To truly test the target sound, students should not get cues from other sources, such as other consonants in the word, different word endings, and so on. With word identification, items in tests had options which differed in the initial letter from the target word. Thus, a student need only know the initial sound to correctly identify the keyed response, rather than actually have knowledge of what that word is.

2. **Not much to read on the reading test.** The amount of text to be read in the tests for all series is quite limited. Counts were conducted on the longest piece of text in each test for each of the series examined.

For all series there were items on tests where a student could have achieved success through means other than the stated objective.

Table 3   Range of Number of Words in Longest Piece of Text

Series	Grade 1	Grade 3	Grade 5
Ginn	6-28	35-70	70-103
Economy	31	107	179-224
HBJ	11-112	50-93	178-217
SF (*Focus*)	15-46	102-134	130-178
Macmillan	6-22	—	—
Holt	8-164	136-574	495-701

As can be seen in Table 3, the number of words in the largest single amount of text to be read within tests was minimal. Holt had notably larger word counts than the other series. These counts were related to the practice of incorporating into the test the requirement that the student read specific parts from the basal readers and answer questions based on those sections.

3. **Inconsistent patterns for items within sub-tests.** For all series, test-developers failed to follow consistent item-specification patterns for the items within a sub-test. For instance, in the Macmillan Level 2 test for Initial Consonants two of the three items have the target sound at the end of one of the options for that item.

Sometimes one of the options for an item is clearly erroneous. At other times none of the options is clearly correct. The latter case is particularly problematic, since students must select as correct an option which is incorrect.

4. **Inconsistency between sub-tests of a unit or Level test.** The pattern of inconsistency is also true for sub-tests within a test. In some instances on a Level or Unit test, items appear to have been generated systematically, while in other sub-tests on the same test no pattern of item generation is evident. For instance, for some vocabulary tests options all begin with the same initial letter, while in others this is not the case. In some instances one test preserves such a system, but in the next sub-test that system is violated.

5. **Making it hard by making it easy.** In some instances by attempting to simplify a task the test-developers have made it more difficult. The Economy Level B test attempts to be flexible in testing colors by using the phrasing "decide which picture shows something which is often [color "x"]. This introduces questions of how much "often" might be. For something that is often green, the choices are line drawings of a carrot with a leafy top, a hand, and a leaf. Since the drawings are black-and-white line drawings, a child could hypothesize that the carrot top is more often green than leaves are, since carrot tops are always green in the supermarket but leaves change color with the seasons.

6. **Problems with illustrations.** Problems with illus-

trations range from the illustrations being simply unrecognizable to something like an ant being depicted when the cue word is bug thus making too much knowledge a dangerous thing. Another problem with illustrations is the variation of sizing within the options of an item set. For instance, a rose may be depicted as large as a child's head. For all but Scott, Foresman, in which directions are variable, teachers are instructed to tell pupils the name of the pictures for phonics items. While this is an attempt to circumvent the criticism of poor illustrations, and the varying background knowledge students may have in naming illustrations, this procedure may not be sufficient to avoid confusing children.

By using simplification of language, test developers often create ambiguities.

7. **Uncohesive and incoherent language.** By using simplification of language, test developers often create ambiguities with cohesive devices which are part of language. The cohesive devices referred to include such things as anaphora or definite/indefinite articles.

In Level F of the Economy series the story is made cohesive by the questions which follow it. Within the story the word "it" is used with no referent.

Ann had a blue pot. She gave it to her grandmother.

"This is for you," said Ann with a smile. "It will get tall."

Grandmother was so glad. She gave Ann one of her new kittens.

6. What was in the pot?
   (a) a plant
   (b) Grandmother
   (c) a smile

7. What did Grandmother have for Ann?
   (a) a leaf
   (b) a pet
   (c) a flag

---

8. **Bubble trouble.** Except for the HBJ tests, developers have opted for the fill-in-the-bubble method of marking answers. Some place letters in bubbles, while others do not, and still others have

Many sets of test items, particularly comprehension items, are not independent.

separate answer sheets. This use of bubbles begins in first-grade and is particularly problematic in the Economy series where this technique (with letters in the bubbles) is used to assess letter knowledge.

8.	ⓐ	c	ⓑ	j	ⓒ	q	ⓓ	s	ⓔ	y
9.	ⓐ	I	ⓑ	o	ⓒ	c	ⓓ	w	ⓔ	L

(Economy, Level B)

9. **Item independence.** Many sets of test items, particularly comprehension items, are not independent. That is, performance on one item is determined by performance on another one. In the Scott, Foresman Level 8 Section 2 (4) test a story is presented, followed by these multiple-choice questions:

What is the main idea of this story?
Which detail did not support the main idea of the story?

If students fail to choose the correct option for the first question, their chances for getting the correct response for the second are jeopardized. Alternatively, a student may be tipped off to the correct response for the first question by looking at the options in the second.

10. **Arithmetic on the reading test.** On some tests knowledge of arithmetic is necessary to successfully select the correct option. For instance, on the Level M test of Economy items require pupils to identify an even number.

In Level 11 of the Holt Unit 4 test subtraction skill is necessary to complete the item which is on reading a graph. A graph depicts how much the Sultan weighed at each of six weeks of a diet. In two items on this test students are asked how much the Sultan lost for a specific week, rather than how much he weighed. Students are thus required to note how much the Sultan weighed at time one, compare it with time two, and find the difference.

11. **Tense confusion.** Grade-one texts often use present tense and avoid other tenses in stories and for questions relating to those texts. In answering the questions the student must decide whether the question asks about the activities that happened in the story or the activities that will happen (*e.g.,* Ginn, Level 4).

Meg and Ned play with Dot.
Dot plays a trick.
Dot runs to the van.
Dot gets in.
Meg and Ned can't see Dot.

4. What does Dot do?
   o sees a truck
   o plays a trick
   o runs to Meg

5. Who runs to the van?
   o Dot
   o Meg
   o Ned

(Ginn Level 4 test)

The reader does not know if a prediction is required or if the question refers to events that have already happened.

12. **Which idea is the main idea?** Lack of clarity as to what constitutes a main idea is involved in a number of items aimed at this objective. In many test items there are a series of chained sentences with no one main idea.

13. **Alternate event sequence.** When pupils are asked to arrange a sequence of events in order there is often a variety of orders possible. For instance, in one test pupils are asked to sequence three events:

Dad will cook the eggs in a pot.
Dad will eat the eggs.
Dad will shop for eggs.

Dad will shop for eggs.
Dad will cook the eggs in a pot.
Dad will eat the eggs.

The language of items is not equally familiar in all American dialects.

Both sequences are possible, since shopping for eggs often follows using them up. This example also illustrates another pervasive problem. The language of items is not equally familiar in all American dialects. Some people shop for eggs and some would use quite different terms to describe buying eggs. This rather urban, middle-class terminology would penalize other learners.

14. **Other problems:**

**Obscure items

(**Whippoorwill** to illustrate the <u>wh</u> sound in Economy, Level F).

**Lack of passage dependency of items on comprehension sub-tests (*see* "Right answers for the wrong reasons")

**Lack of context in items testing context.

(From Harcourt Brace Jovanovich (Level 11) on "Context Clues")

Threads were hanging from the <u>tattered</u> edge of the beach towel.

        ( ) torn   ( ) neat   ( ) repaired

**Formulaeic notions of how to identify story elements such as main idea, characterization, etc. (*see* item 12 above).

**Lack of clarity of the cause/effect relationship.

In some cause/effect items the wording is confusing; in others more than the wording is problematic. Consider these items from the same test:

---

3. We didn't have any seeds, so I <u>bought</u> some.
cause   effect
4. I'm taking care of the corn plants because <u>corn</u> is <u>my</u> <u>favorite</u> <u>vegetable.</u>   cause effect

---

These items seem problematic as exemplars of cause and effect relationships.

**Lack of clarity of the difference between fact and fiction

In Test 4 of the HBJ Periodic Tests there is an oversimplification, if not a misrepresentation, of the difference between facts and fictional details:

(a) Ralph walked toward the door of the committee room. (b) He knew that this was the chance he had been waiting for. (c) Ralph Nader had started speaking out for people's rights while he was still in college. (d) His main concern was the safety of the American automobile. (e) Now, as he approached the committee, Ralph felt nervous but determined. (f) In later years, Ralph Nader would appear before many government committees to tell about the dangers of the American car.

Aside from the major issue of whether these tests are testing what they should test, they are not testing well what they claim to test.

On the lines below, write the letters of the three sentences that state facts.

1. _____ 2. _____ 3. _____

**Problematic directions

Some tests and test items have directions that are ambiguous, are hard to follow, or present possible confusing messages for some students.

These comments are based on an analysis of the tests as the test publishers present them. We looked at them in terms of whether they did what they claimed to do. Further, there are execution problems on every test of every series. Aside from the major issue of whether these tests are testing what they should test, they are not testing well what they claim to test.

Science in the Tests

There is not much evidence of science in the crucial test portion of basal readers. At their best they test some of what is taught, but what is tested is not the whole of reading. They take the form of objective-referenced tests, but they do not meet the recognized criteria for design of such tests. They are, according to their own design criteria, poorly executed. We could not find justification in the tests for the claims publishers make for them, or the use of the results to make decisions about the academic lives of students. Far from

Far from being the scientific core of the basal programs the tests may well constitute their weakest components.

being the scientific core of the basal programs the tests may well constitute their weakest components.

DESIGN AND EXECUTION IN THE BASAL PROGRAM

The same issue that we have explored in the tests can apply to the whole program. There are questionable occurrences in each part of the basal program. Are these the result of the careful application of the principles on which the basal is built? Or are they examples of poor execution? We can assume, for example, that changes made in transforming Judy Blume's book into "Maggie in the Middle" were deliberate. But the illustrator made a mistake in showing Maggie in oversize clothes when the text says the clothes fit her. An editor compounded that mistake by framing questions that require readers to infer that the clothes were too big for Maggie. That's a matter of poor execution.

This example is not a rare one. Many of the execution problems we have illustrated with the basal tests are found in other components of the basal programs. That's particularly true in the workbooks and other practice materials because in many cases the items in the tests are identical in format to the items in the workbooks.

SPANISH-LANGUAGE BASAL READERS

In a study parallel to our study of English-language basals, Freeman examined six Spanish-language basals. All were published in the United States since 1980 except the Santillana series, a program from Spain with American components and a history of popular use in the United States. Addison-Wesley, Economy, Houghton Mifflin, Macmillan, and Scott, Foresman published the other programs. The last is a direct translation of the company's *Focus* program.

Again, though each of the published programs has

some differences, they are more alike than different. Some, for example, appear to approach print differently, using syllabic, word, or multiple cuing systems, but the ultimate goal of the many skill exercises and questions is word identification. Recent reading comprehension theory is discussed in the teachers' materials and comprehension is stressed, but it is clear when the comprehension questions are examined that the materials reflect the idea of comprehension as product and not process.

Like the English-language programs, there is usually one right answer to every question. The text is seen as being the same for all readers, and students are expected to get the same information from the text as the people who wrote the questions.

Students get a simplified, synthetic, and repetitious text that is controlled for word, sound, and/or syllable introduction. Though teachers' guides discuss the importance of what students bring to the reading, there is little recognition in the materials of students' strengths and abilities.

Language in all the series is, with the exception of poetry, adapted. In the Spanish-language basal the adaptation raises an important issue. Several publishers claim that they produced Spanish basals to provide quality Spanish literature. But, in fact, most of the selections are translated from English. Not much of the original literature in Spanish is actually used.

Translation of basal components introduces other problems. "The Mouse in the House," becomes "La Raton en la Casa" so the rhymes are lost. In one lesson tongue-twisters were used; for example, "Tres tristes tigres tragaban trigo en un trigal." But the pictures on the page still relate to the English originals (Focus, Silibidos y Sueños, p. 99).

So, despite their promise, the materials do not provide the kinds of experiences that allow students to encounter the reading process or the richness of Spanish literature. There is the same control of reading, lan-

Their major strength is also their major weakness.

guage, learning, and teaching as in the English-language basals, the same concentration on skills, but not on comprehending authentic language. There is the same narrowing from reader to workbook to test as their English counterparts follow.

In short, what these Spanish-language basals represent is a translation of the same technology the basal industry has produced to Spanish-language reading instruction. Readers of Spanish now also have access to the promised benefits of business and science. And bilingual teachers may submit to the same controlled methodology in both languages.

SO WHAT ABOUT THE BASALS?

In a nutshell we found the basals we examined to be beautifully packaged, copious sets of instructional materials seriously limited by the criteria for design which basals were founded on and to which they still strongly adhere. They still cling to behavioral *Laws of Learning;* they still assume a teacher who is not competent to plan instruction; they still represent an industrial management view of schooling. They are more alike than different.

Basals main strength is their tight organization and sequence. This creates a sense of scientific rigor. Everything is precise, direct, and goal-directed, from the lesson organization to the controlled vocabulary to the complexly labeled questions that precede, accompany, and follow the reading of the stories and other texts. They appear to offer to schools and to teachers the complete programs they have promised.

But their major strength is also their major weakness, because the essential elements of the organization and sequence do not easily permit modification in any but superficial ways. New understandings of the reading process, and new insights into teaching and learning, find their way into the language of the manuals and even into how the system is described, but they do not change the essential nature of the basal or how learners and teachers experience it. They remain locked into the notion that the learning of reading can happen skill by skill and word by word and that learning is the direct result of teaching.

Furthermore, at each point where the apparently tight system and goal-orientation of the basal is carefully examined, there appear to be misconceptions, inconsistency, misdirection, and misapplication. Lessons and test elements do not do what they claim to do. Labels are used inconsistently. And poor execution is found throughout the programs: Mismatching of questions and content, incoherent texts, awkward grammar and phrasing, unreadable text, unanswerable questions. Basals are not in reality what they appear to be. They are not consistent with their own design criteria.

More than anything else basals are built around control: They control reading; they control language; they control learners; they control teachers. And this control becomes essential to the tight organization and sequence. Any relaxation of the control in any of these elements would appear to undermine the whole system. That's why publishers admonish teachers not to wander from the direction of the manuals; that's why administrators issue mandates requiring teachers to be faithful to the program.

If there were evidence that this tight control was necessary to the development of reading, then we might grudgingly tolerate it. But the evidence from science —recent theory and research—is that reading, like all language, only develops easily and well in the context of its use. The learner needs the freedom to experiment, to take risks, to raise questions in the process of trying to make sense of comprehensible written language. Nowhere in the basals are learners encouraged to decide what is for themselves a good story or text. There is little choice, little self-control, little sense of ownership of their own learning and their own reading. That's not just bad for their reading development. It's

A method may help or hinder, facilitate or complicate, but not create learning. (Ferreiro and Teberosky)

also bad for their development as thinkers, as learners, as participants in a democratic society.

What alternatives are there to this passive view of learning built on Thorndyke's Laws of Learning? In *Insult to Intelligence* Frank Smith (1986) quotes sociolinguist Roger Shuy's summary of the research on language learning:

> This research shows that good language learners begin with a function, a need to get something done with language, and move gradually toward acquiring the forms which reveal that function. They learn holistically, not by isolated skills. Such learners worry more about getting things done with language....they experiment freely and try things unashamedly (Shuy, 1981).

Ferreiro and Teberosky (1982) explain Piaget's view of learning:

> The concept of learning, (understood as the process of obtaining knowledge) inherent to genetic psychology rests on the assumption that there are learning processes that do not depend on methods....A method may help or hinder, facilitate or complicate, but not create learning. Obtaining knowledge is a result of the learner's own activity. An intellectually active learner does not necessarily carry out observable activities. An active learner compares, excludes, orders, categorizes, reformulates, confirms, forms hypotheses, and reorganizes through internalized action (thought) or through effective action. A learner who carries something out according to instructions or a model provided by someone is not, usually, an intellectually active learner (p.15).

Research of several kinds, in several disciplines, is producing a view of children as remarkably strong, active language learners. Research by Clay (1975); Y. Goodman (1984), Harste, Woodward and Burke(1984); as well as the Piagetian group headed by Ferreiro, show that children are developing reading and writing before they come to school.

Harste has stressed the need for learners to have a sense of ownership of their own learning processes in developing literacy, a sense that what they are learning belongs to them and that they are in control of their own learning.

Miscue analysis research has shown developing readers at all levels of ability are engaged in trying to make sense of print when what they are reading is comprehensible (Goodman and Goodman, 1978; Goodman and Gollasch, 1980). It has shown that the very errors people make as they read reveal them as actively using the reading process to construct meaning.

Research by schema theorists and cognitive psychologists also shows developing readers as active hypothesis testers drawing on their prior learning as they seek meaning in what they read. Anderson says:

> Reading is a constructive process. No text is completely self-explanatory. In interpreting a text, readers draw on their store of knowledge about the topic of the text...That is to say, readers "construct" the meaning (Commission on Reading, 1984, p. 7).

All this presents the learner in reading as strong and active. This view is at odds with the premise in basals that learners are weak, deficient, and passive, and therefore must be controlled.

Dewey's central concept of learning by doing and Vygotsky's view of learning as the internalization of social activity also depend on learners who are actively seeking knowledge, supported by teachers but in control of their own learning. Pupils with basal readers are not the active seekers of meaning and order depicted by Piaget; they don't learn by doing, as Dewey has suggested, or from participation in social activities, as Vygotsky believed they do.

Shannon says:

> Professionals control their work and make critical judgments about what procedures and materials are most suitable for specific situations (Shannon, 1987, p. 311).

Duffy, Roehler and Putnam conclude:

> As more is learned about the nature of reading and the effective teaching of reading, the need for elementary

The need for elementary school teachers who will make substantive curricular decisions becomes more apparent.

school teachers who will make substantive curricular decisions becomes more apparent (Duffy, Roehler, and Putnam, 1987, p 357).

But just as it must control reading, language, and learning, the basal's central premise requires that it control the teacher. And the control of teachers, far from assuring their effectiveness, limits both their authority and their responsibility for the development of pupils. One of the great tragedies of the basals is the dependency they have built in teachers.

Smith sees this pedagogy as a myth in conflict with "the reality of the brain, and especially of how children learn. Children learn constantly and so do adults —when they have not become persuaded that they can't learn."

The myth is that learning can be guaranteed if instruction is delivered systematically, one small piece at a time, with frequent tests to ensure that students and teachers stay on task (Smith, 1986).

Again, it is not that the authors and editors do not know there are alternatives to their narrow, controlled view of teaching. Holt, in fact, includes in their manual an abridged version of Smith's "Twelve Easy Ways to Make Learning to Read Hard…and One Difficult Way to Make It Easy." His easy ways caricature the common instructional strategy of basals:

1. Aim for early mastery of the rules of reading.
2. Ensure that phonics skills are learned and used.
3. Teach letters or words one at a time, making sure each letter or word is learned before moving on.
4. Make word-perfect reading a prime objective.
5. Discourage guessing; be sure children read carefully.
6. Encourage the avoidance of errors.
7. Provide immediate feedback.
8. Detect and correct inappropriate eye-movements.
9. Identify and give special attention to problem readers as early as possible.
10. Make sure children understand the importance of reading and the seriousness of falling behind.

11. Take the opportunity during instruction to improve spelling and written expression and insist on the best spoken English.
12. If the method you are using is unsatisfactory, try another (Smith, 1973, Holt, p. T132-33).

In the article Smith continues:

> Learning to read is a complex and delicate task in which almost all the rules, the cues, and all the feedback can be obtained only through the process of reading itself...Now I have reached my one difficult rule, the antithesis of the twelve easy rules: Respond to what the child is trying to do.

If the publishers know this, why do they adhere to the narrow model of teaching? The answer is control, again. How can they control teaching unless they make it specific and sequential? Further, how can they justify the basal if good teaching is responding to what the child is trying to do.

Smith suggests that:

> ...the view of language and learning that psycholinguistics promised was superficially examined by the educational planners and set aside as too vague. Notions that children learned best by being immersed in everyday experience did not fit well with the philosophy that believed in quality control and the delivery of instruction to children as if they were on a production line (1986, p. 26).

In fact, the whole justification for an all-inclusive and carefully sequenced basal reader series depends on controlling passive learners. The materials not only dictate what students should do but also how and when they are to do it. That's why the recognition in the teachers' manuals of modern knowledge of language and cognitive development does not get translated into the texts, workbooks, and tests of basals. And it's why when attempts are made to apply holistic concepts, they get distorted and subverted.

In New Zealand the schools have for decades used a much broader learner-centered pedagogy. In *Reading in Junior Classes*, published by the Department of Education, here is what they say about the teachers' role:

The whole justification for an all-inclusive and carefully sequenced basal reader series depends on controlling passive learners.

Basals have in fact become a rigid technology that is highly resistant to change and improvement.

It makes sense to have children behaving like skilled readers to the fullest extent possible from the beginning, and it is the teachers' role to help children develop the [necessary] strategies, understandings and attitudes....

Just as parents and caring adults encourage children to acquire spoken language by taking risks, teachers should encourage children to take risks in reading. Teachers should think of "mistakes" as "miscues" and by accepting children's approximation, assist them in learning the techniques of confirmation and self-correction as aspects of self-improvement in reading....

Teachers should see that they don't rob children of the opportunity to learn for themselves by saying, "That's right" or "That's wrong" but rather, "Well, does that seem right?" and "How can you be sure?"...

Sensitive observation of what a child actually does while reading provides a teacher with information about what a child has understood, what attitudes prevail, and what the child needs to learn next (New Zealand Department of Education, 1985).

This holistic view of teaching depends on a holistic view of the learner and of reading and is in sharp contrast to the controlled view of teaching in American basals.

Clearly, most of the generations of children who experienced the basals over the past six decades have learned to read. Partly this is a tribute to the learners themselves. They learned to read in spite of the flaws in basals and in the instruction based on them. Partly it is a tribute to the teachers who found ways of making the basals interesting and found ways of supplementing or varying their use to fit the needs of learners. And partly it must be due to some aspects of the materials themselves; whatever their faults, they did focus the attention of teachers and learners on reading.

Clearly also the blame for limitations and lack of success must also be shared. The basals have not fulfilled their promises; they have not taught all children to read easily and well. They have not eliminated teacher and learner difference. They have not reflected the best and most up-to-date knowledge of science. Basals have in fact become a rigid technology that is highly resistant to change and improvement.

If the current basals were regarded as one among several alternative approaches to materials for reading instruction then we could assume that those teachers and administrators who prefer them could continue to use them. Others would find alternatives and over time the merits of the competing systems would become clear. The present view of basals locks out alternatives and locks in teachers and learners.

The purpose of this report card on basals is not to suggest that they be immediately and universally abandoned but rather that they are not the best that modern business and science could offer our schools. Our classrooms need to be opened to alternatives. It is time that a broad scale reconsideration of the teaching of reading in schools take place. Such rethinking requires that we also rethink the role and nature of the basal reader. The producers, the users, and the public all need to be involved in this reconsideration.

The present view of basals locks out alternatives and locks in teachers and learners.

7

ALTERNATIVES WITHIN AND WITHOUT THE BASALS

We began this report with a consideration of the premises of the basal reader. The central premise of the basal, we stated, is that a sequential all-inclusive set of instructional materials can teach all children to read regardless of teacher competence and regardless of learner difference. Further we presented evidence that the vast majority of both administrators and teachers accept this premise and go farther by believing that the basal is indispensible to reading instruction and that everything that is in it is there, in the sequence it is found, for scientific reasons.

RECONSIDERING THE PREMISES

In this report we have shown the historical roots of the basal in the American belief that industrial management technology rooted in science could solve all personal and social problems. We located the origins of the basal in the period between the two World Wars when many teachers were poorly trained, few Trade books were available, and most supervisors and administrators knew little about the process, learning, and teaching of reading. Furthermore, as compulsory universal education at least at the elementary level became a reality, the schools were jammed with a full range of students, many of them from semi-literate homes.

It seemed logical and necessary to turn to business in order to bring the benefits of science to teaching American children to read. Behavioral psychology was proclaiming that it had discovered the Laws of Learning and of thinking. The resultant technology, the basal reader, could assure universal learning even without competent professionals in the schools. Times and circumstances have changed since this argument was first advanced, however.

Today's Professionals

Teacher education has come a long way in the sixty years since basals began taking their modern form. American teachers have bachelor's degrees and in many cases master's degrees. Their education includes a broad base in the liberal arts, usually an academic major or teaching major, and substantial preparation in professional courses including some form of student teaching or internship. Teachers are most commonly educated in professional colleges or universities in contrast to the short post-secondary normal school education teachers were getting half a century ago. While the teaching profession has not achieved high status in the public view or shaken off the image of an earlier time, it is comprised of well-educated certified professionals.

A large group of reading specialists has emerged with advanced education in reading. These are the specialists and reading supervisors in the schools. The International Reading Association is one of the largest subject area organizations within the educational profession in North America.

There is little justification for treating today's professionals as incompetent to make instructional decisions, plan curriculum, organize instruction, and locate and make available materials for pupils to read. But basals are still organized around making all the decisions for the teacher. The thick manuals are tightly sequenced and scripted. As a whole, professionals have not challenged the role assigned them by the basals. It may take a generation for teachers to redefine themselves and liberate themselves from the control of basals, even if the role of basals is redefined.

The basal reader has stood authentic reading on its head.

Reading Materials

If one justification for the development of basals was the paucity of children's books available in general and particularly in schools and classrooms, then we need also to consider the explosion of the whole field of literature for children and adolescents since basals made their appearance. From picture story books to realistic fiction to nonfiction to science-fiction and fantasy, children's literature has increased in both quantity and quality. Still, as reported in our discussion of the economics of the basal, schools spend far less money on this vast literature than they do on basal programs. Perhaps the California Reading Initiative, with a strong focus on learning to read by reading real literature, will make a start in changing all this.

We've demonstrated that basal editors and authors do attempt to sample this literature in their anthologies. But we've also shown the process of censorship and revision this literature goes through to make it fit into the basals. The basal reader has stood authentic reading on its head. It has made reading a word-centered sequence of skill development with a synthetic text or a revised and censored selection from literature as a vehicle for students to practice skills and controlled vocabulary. This results in perhaps 10 percent of the time the school devotes to reading instruction actually being spent on reading. Furthermore, for beginners and low achievers, the materials they are asked to read are likely to be the peculiar type of synthetic texts which form a unique basal reader genre. There is a self-fulfilling prophesy here. When young pupils have difficulty with the synthetic texts, that is taken as proof that they could not read natural texts which are assumed to be more difficult because they haven't been synthesized or revised.

Reading programs in other English-speaking countries have demonstrated that children can learn with authentic literature right from the beginning. American teachers have begun to turn to these literature-based programs as one alternative to the American basals.

Science and Business

The science of the basal reader was built in the early days of behavioral psychology. As Graham showed in his study of the making of basal readers (Graham, 1978), the backbone of the basal is the scope and sequence chart. And that is largely derived from Thorndyke's Laws of Learning with their emphasis on sequence, practice, cause/effect, and identical elements.

The industrial management concept which was going to make it possible to teach all pupils to read with minimally qualified teachers has become the key principle in the basal. All aspects—reading, language, learning, and teaching—must be tightly controlled. If new concepts from science—research and theory—are considered, they must be transformed to fit into the requirements of control. So instead of assuring that reading instruction will be scientific, the use of industrial management techniques has frozen the knowledge base of the basal in the 1920s where it began.

There is still a fascination with business management in the United States. In reading, it goes beyond the basal to management systems for controlling use of the basal, to mastery learning programs that control learners and teachers even more tightly than the basals do, and to computerized programmed reading instruction which eliminates the teacher partially or entirely. These are natural extensions of the central premise of the basal. Within the logic of the basal they represent a viable alternative for those who equate reading with test performance and who point to the fact that the basals have not delivered the high test scores they promise.

We lost the learner and the teacher in the quest for efficiency.

These management alternatives are less eclectic than the basals, and in some sense offer more consistent use of their principles. But they also eliminate some of the redeeming features of the basals. Literature often disappears altogether and the time spent reading even revised texts disappears to close to zero as the programs attempt to keep their pupils "time on task" near 100 percent, the task being to respond to sequences of skill questions. The programs also eliminate the humane and professional variability teachers have been bringing to the use of basals.

What the industrial management model has always had trouble accommodating are the human factors. We lost the learner and the teacher in the quest for efficiency. We need to find models that can bring them back.

ALTERNATIVES TO BASALS

Before we consider the issues involved in changing basals we'll explore some non-basal alternatives.

Can Kids Learn to Read Without Basals?

Children growing up in literate societies are aware of and attracted to written language. A fair number of children learn to read before they come to school without any instruction. Durkin (1966) studied American children who learned to read before coming to school. She found a significant number in all populations.

Even those who are not fully readers when they first

Thinking children play an active role in learning written language. (Ferreiro and Teberosky)

come to school already know a lot about the function, form and use of reading and writing. Ferreiro and Teberosky have brought a Piagetian prospective to studying this early development.

> We believe that these thinking children play an active role in learning written language. It is absurd to imagine that four-or-five-year-old children growing up in a literate environment that displays print everywhere (on toys, on billboards and road signs, on their clothes, on TV) do not develop any ideas about this cultural object until they find themselves sitting before a teacher at the age of six. This is difficult to imagine knowing what we know about children of this age, children who wonder about the phenomena they observe, who ask the most difficult-to-answer questions, who construct theories about the origin of humans and the universe (Teberosky and Ferreiro, 1984).

In some cultures, notably in Japan, schools expect children to be reading before they start school. That's because there is a high cultural value placed on early literacy and because children have many authentic experiences with written language.

Can Teachers Teach Reading Without Basals?

Throughout the history of basal domination there have been successful non-basal alternatives which were at least as successful as basals. What many of these programs had in common is a focus on involvement of children from the beginning in reading meaningful materials, often real books for children. Most recently in North America a grassroots whole-language movement has emerged among teachers, at least partly as a result of their rebellion against the narrow controls of the basals. In Canada this whole-language movement has become so widespread that it is now official policy in some school authorities and in some provinces, particularly Nova Scotia and Quebec. Whole-language programs are also strong in England,

New Zealand, and Australia. In whole-language schools and classrooms basals are either de-emphasized or eliminated altogether. De-emphasis often involves using only the pupil's books and using them selectively as sources of stories and articles.

Because it has taken a certain amount of courage, particularly in the United States, for teachers to move away from basals and toward whole language, it is sometimes suggested that only highly competent teachers can do without basals. While we would not argue that success without basals does not require competent teachers, neither can we accept the view that incompetent teachers can be successful with basals or that the control of the basal can compensate for the incompetent teacher.

Several circumstances can facilitate teaching without basals:

1. Simply making it legitimate for teachers to choose not to use basals. Many teachers feel quite confident that they could have successful reading programs if they were not required to use basals.
2. Providing alternative materials for non-basal teaching. Largely this means making funds that would be spent on the basals available to purchase children's literature of a wide variety to establish classroom libraries.
3. Providing staff development and administrative support for teachers to develop non-basal alternatives. Part of the grassroots whole-language movement has been the spontaneous development of support groups among teachers. Many school districts are encouraging such development and supplementing it with central personnel. In many cases successful whole language teachers play key roles in staff development.
4. Refocussing school and district policies so they center on making sense of print and not on gain scores on tests. That means encouraging a wide range of evaluative procedures which go beyond testing skills.

Choosing not to adopt may be the most effective tool basal selection committees have for assuring innovative programs.

CHANGING THE BASALS

As a product of American industry it is clear that the basal reader will not change in any substantive way until the market changes. As long as they are making profits for their publishers basals are unlikely to undergo any important changes. That fact is independent even of the wishes of the editors and publishers themselves. If one publisher took the risk of producing a highly innovative program and it were highly successful in its sales, capturing marketshare from its competitors, there would be a rush to emulate its new features. Or if purchases of all basals fell off drastically and publishers believed this was due to broad dissatisfaction with their products and a shift to non-basal programs then there would be anxious meetings in the board rooms, heads would roll, and policies and products would change.

So the best way to assure innovation in basals is to limit use of existing basals. Nothing else is likely to make much difference. Choosing not to adopt may be the most effective tool basal selection committees have for assuring innovative programs.

SIGNS OF PROGRESS FOR BASALS

The publishing industry does have some precedents to follow in adapting. Below are some worth considering.

Canadian Basals

In Canada, with an extremely strong whole-language movement and different traditions in use of basals and teacher authority, several publishers have produced innovative programs. Among these are Nelson's *Networks* and McGraw-Hill's *Unicorn*.

One program, *Impressions*, is produced by Holt, Rinehart and Winston of Canada. It is presented as a whole-language program. In this context it is committed to moving from whole to part:

With this approach, children first experience and re-spond to the selection as a whole, then investigate the sentences, words, and letters after meeting them in meaningful contexts(Holt, Canada, *How I Wonder,* Teacher Resource Book, 1984. p. 1).

Impressions has the appearance of a basal. It has read-ers for pupils, workbooks, and a teachers' resource book. It also has an anthology for teachers with poems and stories to read to pupils. It has big books, enlarged versions of stories from the pupils' books that are for shared reading, a holistic technique developed in New Zealand. It has audiotapes of literature selections so pupils may hear and follow them. And it has a writing program built into the components. The teachers' re-source book includes a lesson plan built around a whole text, such as "Sing a Rainbow," a song which ap-pears as an early selection in the first level. Key state-ments in the philosophy of the program are:

Reading is a meaning-seeking process.
The language arts should be integrated.
To understand print, the reader uses three kinds of
    information:
…semantic,…syntactic,…phonographemic.
Children need access to print.
Children should have the best language models.
Rhythm, pattern, and familiarity provide language
    hooks for children to hang their ideas on.
Language is a major tool for learning.
Language learning is not a solitary activity.
The children's own language is a major resource.
Children need to be able to use language for many
    different purposes.
Successful and appreciated writing experiences
    should be a natural part of each child's day-to-
    day language activities.
Every child needs to feel that he/she is a successful
    member of the larger group (Holt, Canada, 1984,
    p. 1).

Evaluation in *Impressions* is through masters "to help
    teachers monitor children's development in all

Many American teachers and schools wanting to change but fearful of giving up basals are switching to Canadian imports.

aspects of the language arts, and to plan appropriate instruction." They provide profile checklists. Procedures include miscue analysis, cloze, and comprehension checks.

This Canadian basal retains many aspects of the basals we have examined. But it commits itself to a different view of reading and language. That means more authentic language in the selections in the beginning levels and different kinds of activities and exercises. It redefines the learner also, though some of the control over development is still present. And there is still a tendency to explicitly tell the teacher what to do.

The Ministry of Education in Quebec has requested Nelson and Holt to produce teachers' manuals that delete reference to the workbooks in their programs as a condition for adoption in the province.

Many American teachers and schools wanting to change but fearful of giving up basals are switching to Canadian imports. For 1986-87 the Portland, Oregon, schools adopted *Impressions* system wide. American publishers might respond with similar programs if there were sufficient defections.

The New Zealand Program

The country of New Zealand is a single school authority. For reading instruction it provides a modest 150-page paperback book as a guide to teachers, *Reading in Junior Classes,* and a set of paperback single story books for pupils, *Ready to Read.* These are original stories commissioned from local writers. There are also school journals in magazine format, published several times a year at several grade levels, which contain stories and topical articles of local relevance. Beyond that, teachers are encouraged to use literature and a range of materials. Big books for shared reading are popular. This non-basal approach has been in use in New Zealand for several decades.

Commercial publishers in New Zealand produce big and little books similar to the government-published program. Both the government and commercial materials from New Zealand and similar whole-language materials from Australia are being imported into the United States, and their popularity is growing.

Literature-Based Reading Schemes in England and Australia

Though both England and Australia have had basals similar to those in the United States they have never had the extensive teachers' guides. In recent years, programs have emerged that are essentially literature-based. A recent one from England is *Journeys into Reading*. In the handbook *Journeys into Literacy*, the program author, Moira McKenzie (1986) says:

> This book sets out to provide suggestions for teachers who wish to organize their reading programme with the assistance of a planned series of books, but who are aware of the need to do this within the larger contexts of literacy, in which they use the whole realm of learning and reading possibilities a child can have in school.

Supplementary American Programs

Can programs like those of Bill Martin, Jr., or literature sets like those provided by Scholastic become the new basals? These are resources that have been popular with teachers who rebelled against basals. But they have never been promoted as alternatives to basals. A swing in their direction would send a strong message to publishers.

8
WHO CAN PRODUCE CHANGE?

The current state of affairs in American reading is not the fault of any one group. Publishers are not alone at fault. There is some truth in their claim that they are giving teachers and schools what they want. There is a vicious circle that can not be broken in any one place. Teachers, administrators, teacher educators, researchers, authors, editors and publishers, and the public all must share the blame and must accept responsibility for opening up reading education.

9

RECOMMENDATIONS

TEACHERS

1. Teachers should develop, individually or with others, a clear position of their own on how reading is best taught.
   a. They should continually examine this position as they work with children.
   b. They should examine policies and instructional materials from this professional perspective.
   c. They should keep themselves well-informed about developments in research and practice.
   d. They should communicate to administrators their own professional views.
2. Teachers individually and collectively need to take back the authority and responsibility for making basic decisions in their classrooms.
   a. They need to make their own decisions about how they use materials including—or not in cluding—basals to meet the needs of their pupils.
   b. They need to be willing to take risks while asserting their professional judgments.

3. Teachers, through their organizations, should reject use of materials, including basals, which make them less than responsible professionals.
4. Teachers should communicate to administrators, publishers, and others their professional judgments about what they need in the way of resources.
   a. They should make clear to publishers the strengths and weaknesses of programs as they work with them.
   b. They should plan material purchases with administrators.
   c. They should demand a voice in text-adoption decisions and policies.

ADMINISTRATORS

5. Administrators should focus more on building teacher competence and confidence and less on mandating basals.
   a. With their teachers, they should establish reading and language policies for their schools and districts.
   b. They should encourage teachers to take control of how they use materials and support them in innovation.
6. They should specify to publishers the kinds of instructional resources they need. If consumers can tell the manufacturers of basals they must meet standards for physical durability, they can also tell them that they must meet standards for content and method.

TEACHER EDUCATORS

7. They should refocus teacher education on preparing informed professionals rather than basal technicians.
   a. Pre-service teachers need to have a full understanding of the knowledge base available and the alternative views of teaching and learning reading available.

b. In-service teachers need help in redefining their roles from scripted technicians with the basal to responsible professionals supporting reading development.
8. Teacher educators need to expand their roles as independent critics of all methods and materials, including the basal technology.

PROFESSIONAL ASSOCIATIONS

9. Professional associations need to play a more critical role in raising issues about methods and materials and providing a forum for the profession.
10. They need to examine their own roles in perpetuating the status quo.
    a. They need to encourage critical reviews of basal programs and alternatives in their journals and at their meetings.
    b. They need to avoid economic dependence on publishers of basals and other materials. Publishers should not be permitted and/or solicited to pay expenses of speakers.
    c. There should be conspicuous signs in the exhibit areas of the conventions saying: "The Display of Materials here does not constitute an endorsement of their quality or effectiveness by the association."
11. They should assume the role of advocates for teachers and learners.
    a. They should establish standards for the treatment of teachers in teachers' manuals.
    b. They should establish exemplary policies on teacher participation in the adoption and use of materials, including basals.
    c. They should establish standards for the treatment of learners in basals and other reading programs.

RESEARCHERS

12. Researchers should address questions of use and application of materials, including basals.

13. They need also to establish a two-way dialogue with teachers, so that they learn from teachers as teachers learn from them.
14. Researchers need to take responsibility for use and misuse of their findings.
15. They need to create new methodologies for researching the unanswered questions about teaching and learning of literacy.

AUTHORS OF BASALS

15. They need to rethink their roles in the continuation of basals.
    a. They need to meet among themselves as professionals rather than as members of competing teams and consider how to change the process of development of commercial programs so that they are less resistant to change and more responsive to new concepts and ideas.
    b. They should not permit the use of their names as authors on materials or components of basal programs which they have not substantially written.
16. They should accept the responsibility for building programs which show respect for teachers and learners.

EDITORS

17. Editors need to rethink their roles in the development of basals.
    a. They need to meet as professionals rather than competitors to establish procedures for opening the process of basal production to innovations.
    b. They need to use their professional knowledge about reading, language, learning, and teaching to establish priorities in program development that move beyond purely profit-and-loss considerations.
18. The work that specific editors have done on the components of programs should be explicitly acknowledged in the materials.

19. They need to establish co-operative arrangements with school systems to assure that all aspects of programs are tried with appropriate learners before they are put in final form in the programs.

PUBLISHERS

20. Publishers should stop the practice entirely of revision and censorship now used in transforming children's literature to serve in the basals and other programs. Careful restrictions should be established even for abridgement and excerpting of selections from literature.
21. The amount of time, if any published program is used as directed, that will actually be spent reading authentic language should be prominently displayed on all materials.
22. Publishers should make a commitment to support innovative alternatives to basals and open the process of basal development to take fuller advantage of the knowledge of authors and editors.
23. The contributions of all those who participate in the preparation of any basal components should be prominently displayed on them and it should be clear what explicit role people listed as advisors, consultants, etc., have had, if any.
24. As an industry, publishers should establish standards of ethical practice.
    a. Explicit limits should be established on the use of gifts of all kinds to teachers and others who are involved in making adoption decisions. These limits should include elimination of paid trips and expensive dinners.
    b. Publishers should limit spending on lavish and ostentatious cocktail parties and other entertainments at professional conventions and meetings.
    c. There should be a truth-in-advertising code established, in co-operation with professional associations, to prevent publishers from making unwarranted claims in advertising or in promotional materials.

POLICY MAKERS

25. Authorities, such as state and local text selection committees, should be authorized to make no adoption or to recommend non-basal alternatives for reading instruction.
26. Laws and regulations that favor or require use of basals should be changed so that:
    a. state funds may be used for non-basal materals.
    b. schools may use programs that do not have traditional basal components.
    c. teachers could not be forced to use materials they found professionally objectionable.
27. Truth-in-advertising laws should be made applicable to tests and instructional materials.
28. Programs such as the California Reading Initiative should be launched to refocus reading instruction on reading rather than skills.

IMMEDIATE RECOMMENDATIONS

The Reading Commission makes the following explicit recommendations about basals and their use that can be immediately implemented:

1. Teachers should not be required to use any program they find professionally objectionable.
2. No adoption of any basal should exclude the possibility of teachers modifying its use or using alternate materials and methods.
3. Publishers should immediately discontinue the practice of revising and censoring selections from children's literature.
4. Publishers should change the way teachers are treated in teachers' manuals of basals. They should be addressed as professionals and be supported in their exercise of professional judgment.
5. School authorities should establish criteria for reading instructional materials and make no adoptions if materials offered do not meet their criteria.
6. In all aspects of development, selection, and use of basals and alternate methods and materials the needs and welfare of students must be placed above all other considerations.
7. School authorities, legislatures, foundations, professional organizations, and others should encourage innovation within and without basals through funding research and experimental programs in schools.

REFERENCES

Anderson, R.C., Osborn, J., & Tierney, R.J. (1984). *Learning to Read in American Schools: Basal Readers and Content Tests.* Hillsdale, NJ: Lawrence Erlbaum.

Aukerman, R. (1981). *The Basal Reader Approach to Reading.* New York: Wiley.

Austin, M., & Morrison, C. (1963). *The First R.* New York: Wiley.

Bagley, W.C., Ed. (1915). "Minimum essentials in elementary school subjects—standards and current practices. (14th Yearbook of the National Society for the Study of Education, Part 1). Chicago: University of Chicago Press.

Barr, R. (December 1986). "The influence of basal programs on instructional activities." Paper presented at Annual Meeting of the National Reading Conference, Austin, TX.

Barton, A., & Wilder, D. (1964). "Research and practice in the teaching of reading," in M. Miles, Ed., *Innovations in Education.* New York: Teachers College Press.

Beck, I. (1984). "Developing comprehension: The impact of the directed reading lesson, in R. Anderson *et al.*, Eds. *Learning to Read in American Schools.* Hillsdale, NJ: Lawrence Erlbaum.

Bloome, D., Puro,P., & Theodorou, E., in press, "Procedural Display in Classroom Lessons," Curriculum Inquiry.

Blume, J.(1981) *The One in the Middle Is the Green Kangaroo* New York: Dell.

Bond, G., & Dykstra, R. (1967). "The cooperative research program in first grade reading instruction." Reading Research Quarterly, 2, entire issue.

Boney, C. (1938). "Basal readers." Elementary English Review, 15, 133-137.

Boney, C. (1939). "Teaching children to read as they learn to talk." Elementary English Review, 16, 139-141, 156.

Bormuth, J.R. (1970). *On the Theory of Achievement Test Items.* Chicago: The University of Chicago Press.

Bruce, B. (1984). "A new point of view on stories," in R. Anderson, *et al.*, Eds. *Learning to Read in American Schools.* Hillsdale, NJ: Lawrence Erlbaum.

Callahan, R. (1962). *"Education and the Cult of Efficiency: A Study of the Social Forces that Have Shaped the Administration of the Public Schools."* Chicago: The University of Chicago Press.

Chall, J.S. (1967). *Learning to Read: The Great Debate.* New York: McGraw-Hill.

Clay, M. (1975). *What Did I Write?* Auckland, N.Z.: Heinemann.

Commission on Reading. (1985). *Becoming a Nation of Readers: The Report of the Commission on Reading.* Washington, DC: National Institute of Education.

Coser, L., Kadfushin, C., & Powell, W. (1982). *Books: The Culture and Commerce of Publishing.* New York. Basic Books.

Cremin, L.A. (1961). *The Transformation of the School: Progressivism in American Education, 1876-1957.* New York: Knopf.

Crocker, L., & Algina, J. (1986). *Introduction to Classical and Modern Test Theory.* New York: Holt, Rinehart and Winston.

Cuban, L. (1984). *How Teachers Taught: Constancy and Change in American Classrooms, 1890-1980.* New York: Longman.

Cubberly, E.P. (1934). *Public Education in the United States.* Boston: Houghton Mifflin.

Darling-Hammond, L., & Wise, A. (1985). "Beyond standardized teaching: State standards and school improvement." Elementary School Journal, 85, 315-336.

Dewey, J., & Bentley, L. (1949). *Knowing and the Known,* Boston: Beacon.

Dolch, E.L. (1950). *Teaching Primary Reading.* Champaign, IL: Garrard.

Dolch, E.L. (1954). "Unsolved problems in reading." Elementary English, 31, 329-331.

Dole, J.A., Rogers, T., & Osborn, J. (1987). "Improving the selection of basal reading programs: A report of the textbook adoption guidelines project." Elementary School Journal, 87, 283-298.

Donovan, H. (1928). "Use of research in teaching reading." Elementary English Review, 5, 104-107.

Duffy, G.G., & Ball, D. (1986). "Instructional decision-making and reading teacher effectiveness," in J. Hoffman, Ed. *Effective Teaching of Reading: Research and Practice*. Newark, DE: International Reading Association.

Duffy, G.G., & McIntyre, L. (1980). "A quantitative analysis of how various primary grade teachers employ the structural learning component of the direct instruction model when teaching reading (Research Series No. 80). East Lansing, MI: Michigan State University, Institute for Research on Teaching.

Duffy, G.G., Roehler, L.R., & Putnam, J. (1987). "Putting the teacher in control: Basal reading textbooks and instructional decision making." Elementary School Journal, 87, 357-366.

Duffy, G.G., Roehler, L.R., & Wesselman, R. (1985). "Disentangling the complexities of instructional effectiveness: A line of research on classroom reading instruction," in J. Niles & R. Lalik, Eds. *Issues in Literacy: A Research Perspective* (34th Yearbook of the National Reading Conference). Rochester, NY: National Reading Conference.

Durkin, D. (1974). "Some questions about questionable instructional materials."Reading Teacher, 28, 13-18.

Durkin, D. (1975). "The little things make a difference." Reading Teacher, 28, 473-478.

Durkin, D. (1978-79). "What classroom observation reveals about reading comprehension." Reading Research Quarterly, 14, 481-533.

Durkin, D. (1981). "Reading comprehension instruction in five basal reading series." Reading Research Quarterly, 16, 515-544.

Durkin, D. (1984). "Do basal manuals teach reading comprehension?" in R. Anderson, *et al.*, Eds. *Learning to Read in American Schools*. Hillsdale, NJ: Lawrence Erlbaum.

Durkin, D. (1987). "Influences on basal reading programs," Elementary School Journal, 87, 331-341.

Durrell, D. (1940). *Improving Reading Instruction*. Yonkers, NY: World.

Education Product Information Exchange. (1977). "Report on a national survey of the nature and the quality of instructional materials most used by teachers and learners (Technical Rep. No. 76). New York: EPIE Institute.

Farr, R., Tulley, M.A., & Powell, D. (1987). "The evaluation and selection of basal readers." Elementary School Journal, 87, 267-281.

Ferreiro, E., and Teborosky, A. (1982). *Literacy Before Schooling.* [K. Goodman Castro, Trans.]. Portsmouth, NH: Heinemann.

Finkelstein, B. (1970). "Governing the young: Teacher behavior in American primary schools, 1820-1880." Unpublished doctoral dissertation, Teachers College, Columbia University.

Flesch, R. (1955). *Why Johnny Can't Read: And What You Can Do about It.* New York: Harper and Row.

Flood, J., and Lapp, D. (1987). "Forms of discourse in basal readers." Elementary School Journal, 87, 299-306.

Follett, R. (1985). "The school textbook adoption process." Book Research Quarterly, 1, 19-23.

Freeman, Y. (1986). "The Contemporary Spanish basal in the United States." Unpublished doctoral dissertation, University of Arizona.

Frymier, J. (1985). "Legislating centralization." Phi Delta Kappan, 67, 646-648.

Gates, A., Ed. (1949). *Reading in the Elementary School* (48th Yearbook of the National Society for the Study of Education, Part II). Chicago: The University of Chicago Press.

Germane, C., and Germane, E. (1922). *Silent Reading: A Handbook for Teachers.* Chicago: Row, Peterson.

Goodman, K. (1979). "The know-more and the know-nothing movements in reading: A personal response." Language Arts, 56, 657-663.

Goodman, K. (1986). Basal Readers: A Call to Action," Language Arts, 63, 358-363

Goodman, K.S. , & Gollasch, F.V. (1980). "Word omissions: Deliberate and non-deliberate." Reading Research Quarterly, 16, 6-31.

Goodman, K., & Goodman, Y. (1978). "Reading of American children whose language is a stable rural dialect of English or a language other than English" (Contract no. NIE-C-00-3-0087). Washington, DC: U.S. Department of Health, Education and Welfare.

Goodman, K., & Page, W. (1978). "Reading comprehension programs: Theoretical bases of reading comprehension in the middle grades." NIE Report.

Goodman, Y. (1984). "The development of initial literacy" in H. Goelman, A. Oberg, & F. Smith, *Awakening to Literacy.* Portsmouth, NH: Heinemann.

Graham, G. (1978). "A present and historical analysis of basal reading series." Unpublished doctoral dissertation, University of Virginia.

Gray, W.S., Ed .(1925). *Report of the National Committee on Reading* (24th Yearbook of The National Society for the

Study of Education, Part I). Chicago: The University of Chicago.

Gray, W.S., Ed. (1937). *The Teaching of Reading: A Second Report* (37th Yearbook of The National Society for the Study of Education, Part I). Chicago: The University of Chicago Press.

Greer, C. (1972). *The Great School Legend.* New York: Penguin.

Harste, J., Burke, C., & Woodward, V. (1984). *Language Stories and Literacy Lessons.* Exeter, NH: Heinemann.

Huck C. (1976). *Children's Literature in the Elementary School,* 3rd ed. New York: Holt, Rinehart and Winston.

Huey, E.B. (1908). *The Psychology and Pedagogy of Reading.* Boston: MIT Press (Republished in 1968).

Hyatt, A.V. (1943). *The Place of Silent Reading in the School Program: Its History and Development from 1880-1941.* New York: Teachers College Press.

Jefferson, T. (1893). "A bill for the more general diffusion of knowledge," in P. Ford, Ed. *The Writings of Thomas Jefferson.* New York: Putnam.

Johnson, D.D., & Pearson, P.D. (1975). "Skills management systems: A critique." Reading Teacher, 28, 757-764.

Katznelson, I., & Weir, M. (1985). *Schooling for All: Class, Rate and the Decline of the Democratic Ideal.* New York: Basic.

Lagemann, E.C., Ed. (1985). *Jane Addams on Education.* New York: Teachers College Press.

Leigh, E., Ed. (1868). *Leigh's McGuffey's New Eclectic Primer in Pronouncing Orthography.* Cincinnati, OH: Wilson, Hinkle & Co.

Lortie, D. (1975). *School Teacher: A Sociological Study.* Chicago: The University of Chicago Press.

Luke, A. (In press). "Making Dick and Jane: The Historical Genesis of the Modern Basal Reader." Teachers College Record.

Mathews, M. (1966). *Teaching to Read: Historically Considered.* Chicago: The University of Chicago Press.

Mayer, J. (1986). "Commentary: On reading it right." The Reading Teacher (April, 1976), 629-631. Reprinted in Teacher's Guide, Never Give Up, Level 11, Grade 3, *Holt Basic Reading,* New York: Holt, Rinehart and Winston, T-477.

McDermott, G. (1975), *The Stonecutter* New York: Viking.

McGuffey, W.H. (1836). *McGuffey's Eclectic First Reader for Young Children.* Cincinnati: W.B. Smith.

McInnis, J. Unpublished Response to Report Card on the Basal Reader, NCTE, Los Angeles, November, 1987.

McKenzie, M. (1986). "Journeys into Literacy" *Handbook for Journeys in Reading,* Levels 1-4, Huddersfield, England: Schofield & Sims Ltd.

Moore, D.W. (1985). "Laura Zirbes and progressive reading instruction." Elementary School Journal, 86, 663-672.

Muther, C. (1985). "What every textbook evaluator should know." Educational Leadership, 42, 4-8.

New Zealand Department of Education. (1985). *Reading in Junior Classes with Guidelines to the Revised Ready to Read Series*. Wellington, N.Z.: Department of Education. Published in USA by Richard C. Owen Co, New York.

Osborn, J. (1984). "The purposes, uses and contents of workbooks and some guidelines for publishers," in R. Anderson, *et al.*, Eds. *Learning to Read in American Schools*. Hillsdale, NJ: Lawrence Erlbaum.

Osborn, J., Wilson, P.T., & Anderson, R.C. (1985). *Reading Education: Foundations for a Literate America*. Lexington, MA: Lexington.

Popham, W.J. (1981). *Modern Educational Measurement*. Englewood Cliffs, NJ: Prentice-Hall.

Popham, W. J. (1978). *Criterion Referenced Measurement*. Englewood Cliffs, NJ: Prentice-Hall.

Purves, A. (1984). "The challenge to education to produce literate citizens," in A. Purves and O. Niles, Eds. *Becoming Readers in a Complex Society* (83th Yearbook of the National Society for the Study of Education, Part I). Chicago: The University of Chicago Press.

Ramsey, J. (1987). "The Madeline Hunter model: New faces in old vases." Review of Education, 13, 63-73.

Rice, J.M. (1893). *The Public-School System of the United States*. New York: Century.

Rice, J.M. (1914). *Scientific Management in Education*. New York: Hinds, Noble & Eldredge.

Robinson, H.M., Ed. (1968). *Innovation and Change in Reading Instruction* (67th Yearbook of The National Society for the Study of Education, Part II). Chicago: The University of Chicago Press.

Seashore, C.E., Ed. (1919). *Fourth report of Committee on Economy of Time in Education* (18th Yearbook of The National Society for the Study of Education, Part II). Chicago: The University of Chicago Press.

Shake, M.C., & Allington, R.L. (1985). "Where do teachers' questions come from?" Reading Teacher, 38, 432-438.

Shannon, P. (1983a). "The treatment of commercial reading materials in reading methods textbooks." Reading World, 23, 147-157.

Shannon, P. (1983b). "The use of commercial reading materials in American elementary schools." Reading Research Quarterly, 19, 68-85.

Shannon, P. (1984). "Mastery learning in reading and the control of teachers and students." Language Arts, 61, 484-493.

Shannon, P. (1986a, December). "Class size, reading instruction, and the use of commercial materials." A paper presented at The Annual Conference of The National Reading Conference, Austin, TX.

Shannon, P. (1986b). Unpublished paper, "Teachers' and administrators' thoughts on changes in reading instruction within a merit pay program based on test scores."

Shannon, P. (1986c). "Consensus or conflict: Views of reading curriculum and instructional practice." Reading Research and Instruction, 26, 31-49.

Shannon, P. (1987). "Commercial reading materials, a technological ideology, and the deskilling of teachers." Elementary School Journal, 87, 307-329.

Shannon, P. (1988) Managing Literacy: Reading Instuction in 20th Century America. South Hadley, MA: Bergin & Garvey.

Shuy, R. (1981). "A holistic view of language, "Research in the Teaching of English, 15:2, 101-11.

Smith, F. (1986). Insult to Intelligence: The Bureaucratic Invasion of Our Classrooms. New York: Arbor House.

Smith, N.B. (1965). American Reading Instruction. Newark, DE: International Reading Association.

Soltow, L., & Stevens, E. (1981). The Rise of Literacy and the Common School in the United States: A Socioeconomic Analysis. Chicago: The University of Chicago Press.

Squire, J.R. (1985). "Textbooks to the forefront." Book Research Quarterly, 12-18.

Squire, J.R. (1987). "A Publisher Reports on the Basal Reader Report Card." Unpublished paper presented at NCTE Conference on the Basal Reader in Los Angeles, November, 1987.

Stone, C. (1922). Silent and Oral Reading: A Practical Handbook of Methods Based on the Most Recent Scientific Investigation. Boston: Houghton Mifflin.

Tierney, R.J. (1984a). "A synthesis of research on the use of instructional text: Some implications for the educational publishing industry in reading," in R. Anderson, et al., Eds. Learning to Read in American Schools. Hillsdale, NJ: Lawrence Erlbaum.

Tierney, R.J. (1984b, April). "Research on reading comprehension instruction in basal reading programs." A paper presented at the annual meeting of The American Educational Research Association, New Orleans.

Tierney, R.J. (1985) "Reading comprehension: What is it? Up and over." Teacher's Edition, Focus, Level 7, Grade 3, Glenview, Ill.: Scott, Foresman.

Tully, M.A. (1983). "A descriptive study of the intents of state level textbook adoption." Unpublished doctoral dissertation, Indiana University.

Vygotsky, L. (1978). "Mind in society," M. Cole, V. John-Steiner, S. Scribner, & E. Souberman, Eds. Cambridge, MA: Harvard University Press.

Waldrop, J.L., Anderson, T.H., Hively, W., Hastings, C.N., Anderson, R.I., & Muller, K.E. (1982). "A framework for analyzing the inference structure of educational achievement tests." Journal of Educational Measurement, 19, 1-18.

Wilson, H.B., Ed. (1917). *Second Report of the Committee on Minimum Essentials in Elementary School Subjects* (16th Yearbook of The National Society for the Study of Education, Part I). Chicago: The University of Chicago Press.

Wilson, H.B., Ed. (1918). *Third Report of the Committee on Economy of Time in Education* (17th Yearbook of The National Society for the Study of Education, Part I). Chicago: The University of Chicago Press.

LIST OF BASAL SERIES

Economy Reading Series. (1986). Matteoni, L., Sucher, F., Klein, M., Welch, K. Oklahoma City, OK

Ginn Reading Program. (1985). Clymer, T., Indrasano, R., Johnson, D., Pearson, P.D., Venezky, R. Lexington, MA.

HBJ Bookmark Reading Program, Eagle Edition. (1983). Early, M., Cooper, E., Santeusanio, N., Fry, M., Harris, J., New York.

Heath American Readers. (1983). Bailey M., Barragan, R., Burke, B., Cramer, B., Farmer, W., Flores, T., Hacker, C., Hutchins, P., Jurata, G. Mayeda, N., Smith, K., Stack, L., Wigner, M. (listed as authors and consultants). Lexington, MA.

Holt Basic Reading. (1986). Weiss, B., Everetts, E., Stever, L., Cruickshank, S., Hunt, L. New York.

Holt, Rinehart and Winston of Canada, *Impressions*. (1986). Booth, J., Booth, D., Pauli, W., Phenix, J. Toronto.

Houghton Mifflin Reading. (1986). Durr, W., Pikulsky, J., Bean, R., Cooper, J., Glaser, N., Greenlaw, M.J., Schoephoerster, M. Alsin, Au, K., Barrera, R., Brzeinski, J, Bunyan, R., Comas, J., Estrada, F., Hillerich, R., Johnson, T. Mason, P. Boston.

Lippincott Basic Reading. A Phonic/Linguistic Series (1981). Walcott, C., McCracken, G., Harper & Row, New York.

MacMillan Reading Express. (1986) Arnold, V., Smith, C. New York.

Scott, Foresman *Focus*. (1985) Allington, R., Cramer, R., Cunningham, P., Perez, G., Robinson, C., Tierney, R. Glenview, Ill.

Scott, Foresman Reading. (1985). Aaron, I., Jackson, D., Riggs, C., Smith, R., Tierney, R. Glenview, Ill.

Author Index

Subject Index